ALL Cookies ain't Sweet

A True Childhood Story

Dr. Cassondra "Cookie" Humphrey

Outskirts Press, Inc.
Denver, Colorado

The opinions expressed in this manuscript are solely the opinions of the author and do not represent the opinions or thoughts of the publisher. The author has represented and warranted full ownership and/or legal right to publish all the materials in this book.

All Cookies ain't Sweet
A True Childhood Story
All Rights Reserved.
Copyright © 2009 Dr. Cassondra "Cookie" Humphrey
V5.0 R2.1

Cover Designed By: Breona Moore
Cover Photo © 2009 Dr. Cassondra "Cookie" Humphrey. All rights reserved - used with permission.

This book may not be reproduced, transmitted, or stored in whole or in part by any means, including graphic, electronic, or mechanical without the express written consent of the publisher except in the case of brief quotations embodied in critical articles and reviews.

Outskirts Press, Inc.
http://www.outskirtspress.com

ISBN: 978-1-4327-1136-8

Outskirts Press and the "OP" logo are trademarks belonging to Outskirts Press, Inc.

PRINTED IN THE UNITED STATES OF AMERICA

"Sometimes in life what looks like an end is really a new beginning"

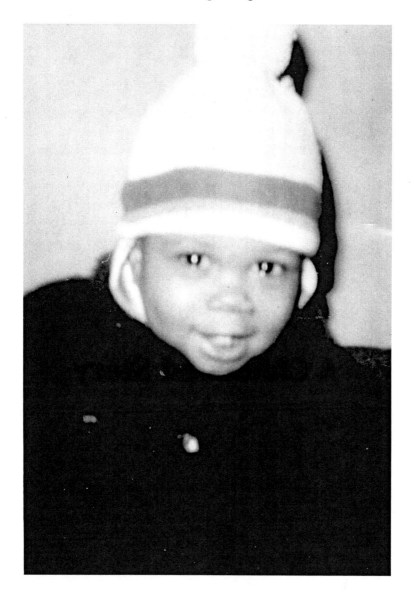

ALL Cookies ain't Sweet

A Childhood Story

In Honored Memory Of

My father, Charles Garner

Grandfather, Alfonso Humphrey

Uncle, Alfonso "Fats" Humphrey

Cousin, Allison "Alie Al" Gray

I Love You.

ALL Cookies ain't *Sweet*

A Childhood Story

DEDICATIONS

First and foremost, I give God all the glory and praise to present my voice in print. **I never could have made it with out you.**

This book is lovingly dedicated to:

My daughter Breona Wennette Moore, you are my life, my joy and inspiration. I forever love you. Special thanks, for designing my book cover.

My brother William Humphrey, where ever you are, I pray that God shields you with his love. I love you.

My foster /God parents and family, Wennie and Frankie Brown, Fern, Paula, and Danny Speller, I love you. There are not enough words to express my sincere gratitude for opening up both your home and *heart to my daughter and I. Wennie Speller-Brown… your love and support was just the dosage I needed to jumpstart my life and I dedicate this book to you.*

Rose Wright-Humphrey (Grandma Humphrey) I thank you for all your prayers. I love you.

My Father Charles Garner (R.I.P.) I love you.

ACKNOWLEDGMENTS

Time to round up the usual suspects:

First, I would like to acknowledge the team members which contribute to the daily success of Future Talent & Entertainment, Future All-Star Basketball Team, and Humphrey House Inc., Tammy Evans, I thank you for being such a good friend. I am forever blessed to have someone like you leading our legal and administrative team. Additional thanks for helping me with the book. Love you girl. Wilner Joseph (Popie) as the team captain, you lead Future All-Stars to higher limits while directing Future Talent & Entertainment's street promotions. You are truly a team player.

Nedra & Roshawn Bryant, my childhood friends. Nedra as my friend and financial advisor you have always went above and beyond. Thanks! Roshawn you are very talented and I thank you for coming up with such a great title for my book...**All Cookies ain't Sweet**.

Kenny, Bonnie and the entire Davis family- thanks for all your love and support over the years. Uncle Buster Gray -- I love you.

To my mentors De'anna Holder-Wade, Sheryl House and Shelia Ferguson, I thank you ladies for sharing all your wisdom, love and support. Nancy McClendon my Mt. Vernon, NY (Mother) you are a beautiful person. My client -- Courtney "Castro" of the- Harlem Wizard, thank you for believing in me. My God children Robin and Amber Lee and Monique Robertson, I love you. Dr. Clifton Bush and Dr. Tuesday Cooper thanks for making my learning experience at Springfield College such a positive one. To my elementary and Jr. high school teachers Mrs. Rawls (Toquam - R.I.P)and Mrs. Berger (Cloonan) thanks, for the extra push, it's one of the reasons why today I'm an Author. Freddie Mouzon we go back Conn, Ave. daze, thanks, for creating my lovely website. Missy P. Brown, I thank you for sharing your publishing expertise.

Lastly, my girls Lisa McCree, Debbie McClintock, Lana Avery and Michelle Grant...we share so many memories and we still have so many years left and I love each and every one of you for who you are and what you will become.

INSPIRED BY YOU

Inspiration is the greatest gift because it opens your life to many new possibilities.

People who truly inspire me have inner beauty. They have overcome major obstacles in their own lives and learned how to accomplish meaningful change.

I Thank You.

Barack Obama
Rosa Parks
Martin Luther King
Wilma Rudolph
Oprah Winfrey
Maya Angelou
Jackie Robinson

Victoria Rowell
Tyler Perry
Cornel West
Bill Cosby
Faith Evans
Keysha Cole
Will Smith
Jamie Foxx
Lisa Price (Carol's Daughter)
Bruce Bowen

TABLE OF CONTENTS

SECTION 1	Coping Mechanisms	1
Chapter 1	Beginning of my Bitter Sweetness	3
Chapter 2	Surviving in the Social & Educational System	9
Chapter 3	Situations	13
Chapter 4	Fighting to Live	17
Chapter 5	Going to Live with Wennie Speller-Brown	27
SECTION 2	Job Corps	37
Chapter 6	Turning Point	39
Chapter 7	New Beginnings	43
Chapter 8	Trying to Keep on Track	49
Chapter 9	Facing the Board	59
Chapter 10	My Graduation Celebration	65

SECTION 3	Moving On	71
Chapter 11	Life after Job Corps	73
Chapter 12	Moving Forward	83
Chapter 13	Love, Baby and Life	99
SECTION 4	Life's Twist	105
Chapter 14	Closure	107
Resources		119

SECTION 1
COPING MECHANISMS

ALL Cookies ain't Sweet

A Childhood Story

CHAPTER 1
THE BEGINNING OF A BITTER SWEETNESS

Being a product of the social service system is how I remember growing up. Born Sandra Gail Humphrey on January 25, 1970, and given the nickname "Cookie". With a name such as sweet as this, one would only imagine sweetness to start off the stages of humble beginnings. However, that was not the case; instead bitter sweet was how it all began. Throughout my childhood and teen age years, I was shuffled around between family members, friends, foster care and group home placements.

I often wonder which direction my life would have taken had I not become a "looked over child" in an inadequate system faced with so many problems and challenges.

Coping Mechanisms

As I reflect back on those years, it feels like a mixture of good and bad experiences. There were so many things that I wish had been different for me, but being so young, things were beyond my control.

It's strange because throughout all my pain and suffering coupled with the trials and tribulations, I knew there was something special about me that set me aside from the rest. I guess you can say I was "cut from a different cloth."

Gifted at birth is the statement which has been said to me and about me, time and time again. I was told God touches every baby that's born, but he touches some a little longer than others, and I believe I happen to be one of those babies.

Learn God's Voice 1 Samuel 3:1-12

Every family has a member that steps up to the plate during a family crisis or situation, in this case it was my grandmother Rose Humphrey the little big mama of the family but everybody called her "Grandma Humphrey".

At a mere one hundred twenty pounds and approximately four and a half feet tall, Grandma Humphrey was the chief and commander from the old school and was a strong believer and enforcer of capital punishment therefore; the consequences of getting out of line were not accepted or tolerated.

Growing up, I didn't believe in her methods of discipline or her tough love tactics, but as a grandmother she stepped up in the absence of my parents. I could only imagine how hard that must have been for her, because she never had a close relationship with either of her children.

The Beginning of a Bitter Sweetness

It wasn't until I became of age, that I realized my grandmother was one of the few positive influences in my corner and her tough love was the only type of love which she knew how to display.

Grandma Humphrey was one of sixteen children, and even though she grew up in a two-parent household with all of her siblings, her relationship with her children and even her grandchildren differ from most. In my opinion, she was just a hard person to please no matter how hard I tried, it was never enough. Thinking back, I now understand her purpose for being so hard on me because it helped me reshape my life towards a positive direction. As I continued to move forward, and although I probably hated to admit it, I noticed I was becoming just like her, a blue print of her if you will. I have developed so many positive traits from her it's somewhat scary at times. I'm sure that's why it was so hard for us to get along because we were so much alike.

I didn't grow up with my father in my life, but because Grandma Humphrey had so many brothers, I had an abundance of great uncles. However, I did have two very close male figures in my life, my grandfather who was my mother's father and my Uncle Fats (my mother's only sibling). I was very close to both of them and spent the early parts of my childhood living off and on with my grandfather. I could tell my grandfather sometimes wished I was a boy because he would always dress me in boy clothes and take me fishing, swimming, to play basketball, and to his favorite spot...the race track. My grandfather was a huge gambler, he betted on any and everything. By the age of seven, I knew how to play every card game that he did. I saw how gambling effected his day-to-

Coping Mechanisms

day living and made a promise to myself to never entertain this type of addiction.

I really adored and looked up to my Uncle Fats and we spent a great deal of time together. He has two daughters of his own Cheri Humphrey and Tammie Briscoe-Humphrey. Cheri and I grew up like sisters and everyone said we looked so much alike. Uncle Fats would often get us confused. He would look directly at me and say come here Cheri and vice versa.

I remember him being such a humble and peaceful individual, who appeared to have very little worries and everything under control. I had no idea he wasn't expected to live as long as he did. A "miracle baby" is what they called him because he was born partially blind and shortly thereafter diagnosed with sugar diabetes. It was by God's miracle that allowed him to see at all, but it was kidney failure that killed him before the age of thirty. My uncle was the link between my mother and me. After my mother moved from Connecticut to New York, he would arrange for us to visit with her via train a few times.

From what I was told, my uncle and my mother were close minus him being a mama's boy and she being a daddy's girl. However, Uncle Fats made a promise to me that in the absence of my mother, he would never let anything ever happen to me and up until death he kept his word. I remember feeling so hurt when he died and somewhat angry at him for leaving me. I felt he abandoned me. I wondered why God would allow such an awful thing to happen to me; first my mom leaves me now my uncle...what's next?

One of the things I remember about my Uncle Fats is he never had a problem speaking up for me no

The Beginning of a Bitter Sweetness

matter who or what the situation was and I always felt safe when he was around. He had the kind of presence that demanded your attention...you know like authoritative. He was also a great listener and always made time to talk to me. Uncle Fats knew that I was very smart, but was more concerned about what was going on in my life at the time. I remember one day we were both at Grandma Humphrey's house and she started yelling at me about something and Uncle Fats yelled back at her and said for her to leave me alone and then he turned to me and said "Sandra, I know you are too young to understand why your mother left you like this, but one day you will." He also stated that my mother and Grandma Humphrey never really got along and that's the main reason she moved to New York, but to always remember that my mother loves me.

This was a lot for a child to digest. It really didn't matter to me what my mother did or what type of drugs she was taking or even how many broken promises she made; she is still my mother and not only did I want to see her, I needed her and I knew that just seeing her alone would ease some of my pain. I was always told that God loves all his children and my mother is no exception. I truly loved her despite her faults and even if it seemed as though she didn't appreciate it, in my heart, she still didn't deserve to be criticized or condemned but comforted and supported because she was weak and fell victim to her addiction and I was determined not to give up on her despite her leaving me the way that she did.

ALL Cookies ain't *Sweet*

A Childhood Story

CHAPTER 2
SURVIVING IN THE SOCIAL & EDUCATIONAL SYSTEMS

After being shuffled around between family and friends I barely knew, I had to learn how to cope with my home life, adult authorities and new rules.

I read that children, who go through the social service system, are less educated and are in worse mental health than their peers. If learning that wasn't bad enough, just imagine how I felt trying to maneuver through new schools, making new friends, while trying to develop socially, and at the same time trying to cope with my new home life, adult authorities and new rules.

I was always labeled the class clown and did many different things in school to get attention, but

Coping Mechanisms

because of everything else going on in my life, school was definitely at the bottom of my priority list. I never did my homework or participated in class activities and the funniest thing is that I always sat in the front row. So eventually school officials suggested to my grandmother that I should go into a special education class for slower students who need more one-on-one attention. I started thinking to myself do they mean the classroom where all the students catch the little yellow short bus? Picture that.

I have to admit I was not one for much conversation, so I can see why they suggested that as an alternative to my learning ability. After skipping my English class for three days in a row, I finally decided to show my face; however it was just my luck it was on a quiz day. I just shook my head and thought to myself damn as I took my seat. I was the last one in and the first one to complete the test. I even had the nerve to stand up with such confidence after never reading any of the books or materials, but English was one of my favorite subjects. I turned in my paper and the teacher said "you can't possibly be finished," and I just smiled while I was gathering up my belongings to leave the classroom, the English teacher then asked me where was I going and I replied "home". I had already taken the test and I didn't feel there was any reason for me to wait around for everyone else to finish especially when I am only seen in her class on occasion and they are there everyday.

The next day I went to class and the teacher asked to speak with me out in the hall. I automatically assumed it was because of my class attendance, when in fact, she informed me of my test score and it just so happen I scored the highest in the class. She knew I didn't cheat because she spent the entire

Surviving in the Social & Educational Systems

time watching me take the test. She just wanted to know why I wasn't taking advantage of my high school education.

I told her that I didn't like school and I was faced with bigger issues in my life and felt school was a waste of time. It's not like I couldn't do the work, I just didn't put forth the effort. I had so much going on in my life at the time and school was not my main priority. Not only that, I had a hard time trying to stay focused and because I was always so anxious, that made it difficult for me to sit still in class.

Needless to say, the school contacted my social worker who later told my grandmother that they thought I was slow and needed to be placed in the special education class. No one ever took the time to ask me what was wrong with me and had they did, they would have discovered that my problems weren't educational but emotional. This has led to some of my behavioral issues that caused me to eventually shut down. In order for me to get everyone off my case about me being slow and putting me in the special education class, I took the test only to prove to everyone I didn't have a learning disability and not only did I pass the test, I received exceptional scores. I sat back and laughed at those so-called experts, because they tried to diagnosis and/or label me with ADD/ADHD when I didn't have it and because of my test scores, this was no longer an issue.

ALL Cookies ain't *Sweet*

A Childhood Story

CHAPTER 3
SITUATIONS

It seemed like no matter how hard I tried to stay away from trouble, trouble always had a way of finding me, and walking away from it came very difficult for me. Even though I came from a pretty large family, I was still an only child and spent a great deal of my childhood fighting to survive.

I guess I can say that due to all of the sport activities my Grandfather introduced me to, I became very athletic. Weighing only ninety-two pounds, I ran track, played basketball, and took up swimming and kickboxing for a few years. My peers thought because I was so small that I was an easy target, but that was absolutely not the case...you know that old saying "don't let the size fool you."

After researching my family history, I later learned that my mother and I have similar behavioral traits.

Coping Mechanisms

Both of us developed a pattern of holding things inside until we eventually explode. This is very unhealthy.

I didn't realize the amount of pain I was carrying around for so long. I was a walking time bomb just waiting to explode. It felt like I was fighting to live and living to fight. I was seeking to be heard and needed attention but I wasn't sure how to go about getting it.

I remember being in the seventh grade at Cloonan Middle School when I had an argument with one of my classmates and she decided to tell her cousin who went to Stamford High and she came to Cloonan to fight me. I had never seen this girl before in my life, but I thought to myself you left school to come see me about some he say she say mess then you deserve everything that I'm about to give you.

She asked if I had a problem with her cousin and at the time, I wasn't sure who her cousin was and honestly I didn't even care. I told her that I didn't know her cousin and for the record I probably had a problem with some of everybody in that school, including her and I proceeded to walk away.

Back then I ran with a few girls from Merrill and Connecticut Ave, Lisa Perry, Pillar Benjamin, Starr, my cousin Ali-Al (God bless the dead) and the twins Raymonda and Amanda (my girls). The twins and I went to the same school and Ramanda and I took some of the same classes together. We both experienced some of the same personal issues so yes you can say we were thick as thieves. The twins weren't always there when I called but they were always on time, and on this particular day they were front and center to make sure no one jumped me.

My Uncle Fats got tired of me getting into so many fights and wanted me to have some protection so he

Situations

gave me a silver ring that resembled a bulls head. I loved that ring, but it was too big for me so he had it sized and added two metal pieces as horns on each side of it. The horns on the ring were extra sharp and the ring was now considered a weapon. Uncle Fats showed me how to use it and explained I could hurt someone with it and possibly go to jail if I get caught with it. So I mostly wore the ring with the horns on the inside of my hand so no one can see them.

 I lived with Grandma Humphrey in River Haven which is an apartment building directly across the street from Cloonan Middle School. Any time I was fighting someone from school or if someone came up to Cloonan, most of my fights took place in the front of my building. Grandma Humphrey would normally be in the window or if she heard that I was going to have a fight she would be waiting for me outside. She could often tell by the size of the crowd that I was somehow involved. On this particular day, this girl decides to follow me to my building and a few words are passed back and forth between us and the crowd started yelling "hit her Cookie." I could see my grandmother in the window out of the corner of my eye shaking her head in disappointment. This type of behavior was common and if I went a full week without fighting that was not normal for me. Grandma Humphrey called for me to come upstairs, but the crowd was so loud I eventually tuned her out. I swung first and then I drop kicked her to the ground. I then turned my ring so that the metal horns were facing upward and I hit her in the face a few times. The ring tore some of the skin off her face and she started to bleed. The crowd started yelling that I had a knife when in fact I didn't; it was the ring my Uncle Fats gave me.

Coping Mechanisms

At that point they tried to stop the fight but they couldn't stop me; I was already in my zone and could not be stopped that easily. Whenever I got like this I became very strong and out of control, almost as if I floated outside my body. After they pulled us apart, I was thinking to myself this girl is older than me and her cousin and she should be setting a better example, but instead she ended up at my school looking for a fight. I knew I was going to beat her, the question was how bad?

Nevertheless I laid hands on this girl and beat her as if she stole something from me and afterwards I had no remorse. My grandmother was in the window watching everything and she was very disappointed in me. I have never seen or heard of this girl before that day but she knew who I was and she still came to my school to confront me. Well needless to say this girl and I became very good friends and to this day we really can't remember why we were fighting in the first place.

At this point in my childhood I had basically given up. I was tired of trying so hard and nothing really mattered to me anymore. Many of my actions were defined as juvenile and I had been labeled a troubled teen. I felt that I had good reason to display this type of behavior and all the therapy in the world wasn't going to cure what I had experienced or what I was feeling inside. I come from a very dysfunctional family and they were good for sweeping problems under the rug; and me being the black sheep of the family, would always take the verbal approach. My seditious actions brought shame and embarrassment to my family, but, that was the only time my family would pay attention to me and I was determined to make noise until someone was ready to listen to what I had to say.

CHAPTER 4
Fighting to Live

After over a dozen fights, misbehaving in class and numerous school suspensions, I was kicked out of the Connecticut school system. Somehow I managed to get kicked out of school and became homeless all in the same day. Grandma Humphrey has put her foot down and has had enough. She told me that she can't do it anymore so she called my social worker to come and pick me up.

I know this was probably one of the hardest calls Grandma Humphrey ever had to make, but at this point, I didn't even care anymore. I was just as tired of her as she was of me, so maybe it was the best thing for the both of us. Grandma Humphrey was very strict, but what I couldn't understand is why she was that way when my great grandmother (Grandma Baby) didn't raise her in such a strict environment.

Coping Mechanisms

I will be the first to admit I was very hard headed, and had I spent any more time at Grandma Humphrey's, one of us would have gotten hurt because she didn't understand me and I certainly didn't understand her.

My social worker was a very nice educated Jewish lady, but had no concept about the black family. This wasn't something that could be taught in any college textbook. Nevertheless, she always tried to accommodate me and my family regardless of the situation or circumstances.

A few days later, I went to stay with a relative in New York. I wasn't there long, but long enough to get into a fight with a girl in the lunch room. Once again, trouble following close on my heels no matter how hard I try to escape it. This was my third week in school and this girl put her hand in my lunch plate...how gross is that? I've always considered myself to be someone who blends in well with others. With all the moving around I did one would have to be adjustable and adapt to survive in any environment.

The girl's name was Stacey and I thought she had to be crazy as hell to put her dirty hands in my plate so I cleared my plate and used the tray upside her head. I hit her twice and the second hit knocked her unconscious, and I continued to kick her while she was out cold. The staff came and I informed them of what happened so did the witnesses at the table.

Well, needless to say the school didn't appreciate my actions and after they reviewed my school records, they weren't interested in hearing my side of the story. I was immediately suspended and my social worker had to make an emergency trip to New York, to get me.

Situations

My social worker made some phone calls and pulled some strings with the Board of Education in Connecticut and pleaded with them to give me another chance and she also informed me that this would also be my last chance. We had a long talk and set some short and long-term goals for me, which I committed to following. I truly believe my social worker felt that I was trying and I explained to her how hard it was for me but I would continue to try. She respected my honesty and told me to work on my temper and to stop letting others bring out the worse in me. One of the reasons I believe we got along so well is that I was always honest with her and I told her what I was going to accept and what I was not.

Grandma Humphrey and my social worker had previously spoken about what happened in New York, and about the goals she wanted to set for the entire family. She also informed my grandmother that in order for us to live together, we must first learn how to work out our differences. I always felt that my grandmother didn't care much for me because I looked so much like my mother and they never really got along with one another.

Grandma Humphrey also had other granddaughters and she treated them differently than she did me and that often made me sad and uncomfortable.

Grandma Humphrey agreed to let me come back home but only under her conditions which were to attend school regularly, respect her and her house rules and stay out of trouble. To be honest, I was starting to get tired of my own actions and I really wanted to change...it was definitely time for a change. I saw how my behavior was affecting Grandma Humphrey's health.

Coping Mechanisms

I knew deep inside my grandmother wanted to save me but just didn't know how to communicate with me so instead she prayed and put it in God's hands. I also knew the guilt my grandmother carried around in her heart for the absence of my parents and I truly believe she wanted to do right by me. Despite all my other failed attempts in the past, I was determined more than ever to keep up my end of the agreement to stay out of trouble and attend school but Grandma Humphrey didn't make it easy for me. She was difficult to please and everything I did just didn't seem to be good enough for her. Every chance she had to beat me, she did and eventually I got tired...enough is enough. So one day, I placed a call to my social worker to remove me from my grandmother's house because I knew eventually I was going to physically hurt her and that was something I didn't ever want to do.

My social worker asked me if I wanted to go live with any other relatives or friends and I yelled out hell no! And we both laughed. I wanted to get as far away as I could, so she found an all girls group home in Waterbury, CT and that was the first time I had entered a residential facility. I didn't know what to expect because I had heard so many different stories. My social worker wanted me to go see it for myself so she took me to go see it. The group home was beautiful. It was an old mansion and the people were very nice. I completed my paperwork and moved in a few days later.

My roommate was a girl from Stamford. I didn't know her but she knew me and we got along fine. She was two years older than me and kept me informed on the house rules, the residents and the staff. She had been there for a year so she also knew her

Situations

way around the city. I had only been in the group home about a month when I overheard some staff members talking about the possibility of the group home closing down. I couldn't believe it and to think they had the nerve to still be accepting new residents. Within two months or so of my arrival, we were told that we were getting another new resident, but never mentioned her name. When the door bell rang I was shocked to open the door and see my girl Lisa McCree standing on the other side of it. Lisa and I met through her brother Todd McCree who was a childhood boyfriend of mine. Lisa and I were very close and considered each other blood sisters.

Lisa and I haven't seen each other for quite some time so we had a lot of catching up to do. Lisa and her mother didn't always see eye-to-eye and last we spoke her mother was sending her to a boarding school, but instead she ended up in Waterbury at the group home. Lisa's mother didn't care for me too much and like most of my friend's parents, she thought I was a bad influence so she didn't approve of us hanging around together. I am sure it was a bit much for her to swallow to see me open the door, so you can imagine how she felt when she saw me. I thought to myself this group home will never be the same with Lisa, Burney and me, oh yes...we're taking over.

Things were finally starting to seem normal for me. I actually liked the group home and was doing very well in school. The group home had a point system and you earned points based on your chores, grades, and overall performance. I always kept high points because it allowed me to have extra phone time and weekend passes. The rumors continued to surface about the group home closing and I got the feeling

Coping Mechanisms

that this was more than just a rumor. So I questioned the staff members on a few different occasions and never received a direct answer. I finally asked my social worker who really wasn't sure but wanted a definite answer as well. A few more months went by and we finally received the verdict that the group home was in fact closing because of financial hardship.

I felt I was a bit young to have a spiritual bond with God but I knew He existed and we needed to have a one-on-one conversation at this point. The closing of the group home not only affected me, but some of the staff members as well. There were staff members living there with small children and six other residents, so basically we were in a residential shelter about to be homeless with in the next sixty days.

I slowly started to slip into a state of depression. I was afraid of the unknown, but ready to take on whatever I was about to face. I knew my options were very slim so I had to come up with something really fast. Even at a young age I was a quick thinker so I decided I would delay the process by faking an overdose. I know what you are thinking...how stupid right? Well they say desperate times call for desperate measures. So I took a bottle of pills and scattered them around me and laid there waiting for someone to find me. I prayed that my girl Lisa would be the one to find me because she always wanted to be an actress too so I thought this would be the perfect opportunity for her to demonstrate her skills.

After lying there for about five minutes or so, Lisa came upstairs and let off a loud scream that I will never forget. She screamed Help! Help! While asking me if I was ok. Of course I didn't respond...instead I acted as if I was out of it. The rest of the staff and resi-

Situations

dent's ran yelling "somebody call 911". The ambulance arrived and took me to Waterbury Hospital.

I had put this plan together so quickly, I really didn't have a chance to think it through because once I got to the hospital my plan started to back fire in more ways than one. After having my stomach pumped for pills that I didn't even take, I was evaluated by doctors and moved to the crazy ward. Yes...the peanut farm. I ended up staying there for about three months, but wait it gets better...Lisa didn't have any idea that I was acting and never took the pills but she did. Lisa took the pills and ended in the hospital and then the peanut farm with me. I was glad to see her but felt responsible for her being there. Here we were two best friends all dressed up with nowhere to go sort of speak. The hospital now thinks we're both crazy...hell for a brief moment, I started to second guess myself but I was desperate at the time.

Once Lisa was feeling better I had to tell her the truth about the pill incident. Even though I have thought about killing myself before, I never had the heart to follow through with it. Lisa admitted that she really took them and said if I was dying she would want to die with me. During my undergraduate studies in Social Services, I learned a great deal about psychology and human behavior. I also learned that what we often say or do is not always what we mean; therefore, if I say I'm going to kill you don't mean that I will literally do it.

Grandma Humphrey and my Mother taking a brisk walk

My mother Jumedia and Uncle (Fat's)

My Grand Parents, Mr. and Mrs. Humphrey

Grandma "Rose" Humphrey

ALL Cookies ain't *Sweet*

A Childhood Story

CHAPTER 5
GOING TO LIVE WITH WENNIE SPELLER-BROWN

While I was in the hospital I had a lot of time to think about me, my life and everything else. I wrote all the time; it was one of the only things that kept me sane during my stay. I was confined behind grey walls with twenty-four hour security, somewhat like jail. I used most of that time to write poetry, songs, and rhymes. I also wrote and kept in touch with my soon to be foster/God sisters Fern and Paula Speller. Fern is about one year older than Paula and Paula is one year older than me, and Danny my brother is two or so years under me. I always had fun being with them we hung out on Conn, Ave, partied at Yearwood Center and always went out of town to have more fun. I loved Wenne Speller, their mother

Coping Mechanisms

and my foster mother. Wennie was different than most mothers, you could actually sit down and have a conversation with her about your problems, and actually talking to her was like talking to Dr. Ruth. She always knew what to say to cheer me up and make me smile. I would often run away from home to stay with them, of course they had no idea I didn't have permission to stay for days at a time, but then again, maybe they did and just never said anything. Wennie knew my situation at home and she often would say to me, "Cookie you know my door is always open" and I knew she really meant it.

When I left to go to the group home, I really didn't tell anyone I just left. I finally wrote Paula to tell her what happened and where I was. During my stay in the hospital, the group home closed and the residents got shifted and split up between different group homes. Wennie found out about this and contacted my social worker to find out if she could get legal custody of me.

By this time I was awarded to the State so there were certain channels and procedures that needed to be followed. I remember speaking to Wennie and she told me the good news of me coming to live with her family. I cannot tell you how excited I was after hearing this news. I remember when my social worker came to pick me up to bring me home. I always thought I wanted brothers and sisters until I got some. But like most siblings we would argue and fight and got on each others nerves, but we also loved each other and had a lot of fun too.

We did everything and went everywhere together. We had a female rap group called the Ladies of the 80's and I wrote my rhymes and free-styled too.

Going to Live with Wennie Speller-Brown

Wennie was soon to marry her hometown sweet heart Fankie Brown. I was very happy that she had someone special to share the rest of her life with. Frankie is my daughter Breona's Godfather and has been a good father figure to all of us.

Wennie never used the term foster mother or referred to me as her foster child, she called me her daughter. I called her my Godmother because she was the chosen one, the one person that God had chosen to guide my life; you know...kind of like my guardian angel. Everything she did came natural and easy. For example, she was a single mother raising her three children and that never prohibited her from taking me in and making me feel like a part of her family.

Although I came from such a huge family I really can't recall many of them stepping up the way she did. I know you have heard that saying "blood is thicker than water"...well I will have to agree to disagree that it's only a phrase used when it's convenient to the situation. I believe family is what you make it and whomever you choose to make it with. I have been embraced by strangers and shunned by family members.

I was finally at peace with myself and the memories and thoughts of my mother were starting to fade away. I wasn't sure what was going on but, so much time had past without me seeing her or being around her, that I started to forget who she was and what she looked like. I would often travel with my mother's Bible which was given to me as a child, and inside I kept a picture of her and no matter how many times I moved or where I moved to, her Bible always stayed close to my heart.

I had always been a critical thinker and lived my life preparing for the worse. I knew there was a strong

Coping Mechanisms

possibility that my mother may never come back for me. Despite all the rumors and/or stories I was told, I couldn't help but wonder if someone had kidnapped my mother and took her far away or maybe I moved so much she didn't have my new address or maybe she's sick or hurt in the hospital. I was old enough to think for myself and embrace my own emotions, but what I couldn't understand is how could any woman have children and leave them and never look back.

Even though things in my life were looking up for me, it didn't change the fact that I was angry inside and I wasn't sure why. It was almost as if I didn't deserve to be happy. I was so use to everything not going in my favor; it was difficult for me to accept change. So what did I do? I sabotaged the situation by getting into a fight. Even though I didn't start it, I didn't try to walk away from it ether, I reacted negatively. I didn't care about the consequences or that this was truly my last chance in the public school system.

I remember seeing the look on Wennies face when she asked me about being suspended. I knew that if the school didn't tell her, Paula would, so I explained what happened and I could tell she was hurt and upset with me. One of the rules she told me early on was I had to remain in school. My social worker was later informed and I could tell from the tone of her voice she was not pleased at all with my actions.

Once again my social worker was there to provide solutions and options. She was known for doing her research and making good on her promises. In other words, she always came through for me. She gave me some information on a program called Job Corps which is a residential vocational training program for

Going to Live with Wennie Speller-Brown

inner city youths. I had heard about the program before but I wanted to learn more about it.

It finally came to me I wanted so desperately to please everyone else that I totally forgot about me. As a direct result I continued to fail myself and I understood early on that the reasons for my situation were beyond my control. It's not like I asked to be placed in these situations but somehow I became a victim twice.

Wennie was the total opposite. Being a mother of three not only made her strong, but responsible as well, and being raised by a strong mother (Grandma Watt) who provided her with the necessary tools to not only be a wonderful mother, but a role model to us all. She never thought twice about taking advantage of me or my situation...instead she did everything that she agreed to and more.

As I got older and moved away, time and distance came between us. I do believe in seasons and feel that Wennie entered my life during that particular season for a special reason and I am truly blessed and contribute my positive success and well-being to her. I will always be forever grateful to my foster mother for stepping up and being such a super woman. In addition to loving me, she made additional room in her heart and a home for my daughter Breona Wennette Moore who I named after Wennie.

There are millions of foster parents who have a passion to provide the day-to-day care for a child and do an excellent job but because of the negative feedback mentioned about the bad foster parents, the good ones are often overlooked. Foster care is provided for children whose families are temporarily unable to care for them. There are over 500,000 children in the U.S. who currently reside in some type of

Coping Mechanisms

foster care. However, African-American children make up approximately two-thirds of the foster care population and remain in care longer.

Yes, I wrote 500,000 and still growing. Despite the increasing numbers, children in foster care and foster care parents lack many needed support and resources. Neglect and abuse have been the leading causes for such an increasing number of young children placed in foster care. Considering everything which took place before living with my foster mother, my health was great and social development skills were as normal as one in my shoes could be. While every effort should be made to make foster care a positive experience and a healing process, I also believe that it takes a special person to be a foster parent or any form of guardian for that matter. The person(s) for this role needs to be able to assess the child's needs, advocate on the child's behalf and most importantly, be loving, patient and understanding.

My foster mother Wennie Speller. Isn't she lovely?

Family Ties
The Brown & Speller Family

Fern, Danny, and Paula Speller.
My foster sisters and brother.

Meet the Browns - My Foster Parents.

Dear Wennie Speller-Brown,

Please accept my poem as a token of my love and dedication to you. I Love You! Mom...

You came just in time to ease my pain,
I was a teenager filled with so much rage,
Yet you showered me with love,
Day after day,
Opened your home for me to stay,
I didn't have your last name,
But that still was ok,
You treated me like family,
Anyway,
You taught me how to pray,
You said believe in God,
He will make a way,
Hold my head high,
Keep my faith,
And it's because of you,
Today I'm doing great,

Love, Cookie

SECTION 2
JOB CORPS

ALL Cookies ain't *Sweet*

A Childhood Story

CHAPTER 6
Turning Point

It would be fair to say that this would be the start of the turning point of my life. For many it was either jail or buried six feet under, but for me it was Job Corps that saved my life and it was also my last hope. It provided me with an alternative to obtain my education and to start my life over. I was eager to make a change. I know this may sound like a broken record but this time it was different. I meant it and I was ready to backup my words with action. I had goals and dreams to one day write poetry, songs, stories, and even the book you are reading right now. The chance to be in a new location, meet new people, and try new experiences started to sound better and better by the second.

I have been through the New England and the Tri-State areas but I had never been as far north of

Job Corps

Waterbury, so when my social worker said the campus was in Chicopee, Massachusetts. I immediately asked her how far that was from Stamford, Connecticut and New York. She informed me that it was about two and a half hours by car and little over three hours by train. I knew that was too far to commute back and forth everyday and for a quick second I thought about how would I get to see my friends. Then I realized that I had to put me first for a change which was my reasons for leaving in the first place. My social worker had a way of convincing or selling opportunities to me. I guess that's what made her so unique, however she had pretty much sold me on the program, and I just wanted to meet with a counselor to be more informed.

I was fifteen the day I enrolled in Job Corps, but the age requirement is sixteen. I registered in December, even though my birthday came in January. I met with a counselor, watched some videos and completed the necessary paperwork.

The Job Corps admissions counselor set me up for a visit to see the campus and to meet with the staff and students. A week later, my social worker and I went to visit the campus and I must admit it was a peaceful ride with a nice clear view, it was December and the leaves were colorful and the trees were huge, not what I was accustomed to seeing in the city.

My social worker and I talked the entire ride mainly about my grandmother because she was in the process of relocating to Georgia. My grandmother had recently buried her only son (Uncle Fats) and was out of touch with her only daughter (my mother) for quite some time, so she felt she really had no reason to stay up north. At this point my grand-

Turning Point

mother felt I needed more than she could provide to me when in fact that wasn't the case at all. I needed and wanted my grandmother to have faith and believe in me...but being honest with myself, how could I ask her for something that I didn't even give to myself? I was now headed in the right direction because I'm enrolled in school and taking control of my life and my actions.

Finally we arrived at the center and it was everything that I imagined it would be and then some. It was a huge facility that almost reminded me of a college campus. A counselor greeted us outside to take us on our tour. The center was divided into sections with girls, boys, and co-ed dorm rooms. I got to see the campus at large, including my soon-to-be dorm room. I met with teachers, vocational instructors, students and administrative staff who all shared both positive and negative views and opinions about the center and the programs that are offered. This was my last chance, so I had to remain positive because I was determined not to fail.

ALL Cookies ain't Sweet

A Childhood Story

CHAPTER 7
NEW BEGINNINGS

I was very excited about my new beginning at Job Corps and my first day to report was scheduled for the day after my sixteenth birthday, so I was able to celebrate with my friends and family and still have time to say goodbye. Fern, Paula, Jennifer and I went to our favorite spot and let's just say Uncle Dave was bartending. We had a good time talking about the past and the future, and aside from me wanting to be one of the Mary Jane Girls. Remember them? - Candy, JoJo, Cheri, and Maxi. Anyway, everyone knew I was talented and had the potential to be whatever I wanted to be in life and they encouraged me to give it my all.

My cousin Kim Robertson was always a great influence in my life. I believe we're second cousins. Anyway our grandmothers on my father's side were sis-

Job Corps

ters. Growing up, I always looked up to her as my bigger sister. Kim had her own style and forever stayed fly with the latest hairstyles and wardrobe. Her mother, my cousin, whom I call Aunt Deet, was the queen of the Robertson family. Big Mama was the one who connected me with the Garners which is my father's side of the family. I had given her the name Big Mama because once she got back on her feet she was the glue that held her family together and she always opened her doors to any and everybody...and I do mean everybody. It didn't matter to her that she had six children of her own, in addition to adopting her brother who died son- Kim who is the oldest, Lynell, Harv, Robin, Terri, Demesha and Kelvin. Aunt Deet's younger brother and sister, Uncle Bam and Aunt Darlene had also played an instrumental part in my life.

    I stayed with Robertson's for about a year or so and we too were also raised together like brothers and sisters. I guess you can say were cousins/brothers and sisters, if that makes any sense. I always admired my cousin Harv's swagger and not to mention what he could do with a basketball on the court. He was the big brother I never had. To this day, we still share that special bond.

    It was something about saying goodbye that I really didn't care much for. I'm not sure if it's because I said it so many times or it was said to me.

    Alan Dantzler, another cousin whom I shared close ties with, was also like a big brother to me. Alan is my cousin on my mother's side; his father was my grandfather's great uncle. Together we shared a lot of commonalties. Somehow, separately, the two of us were heading down the wrong path. Alan was blessed with a beautiful gift; he knew how to play the

New Beginnings

piano like an angel. Now that I think about it, this could have been his ticket out the hood because he was just that good.

Starr Baynes-Merritt was another one of my big sisters. We both went to church together and I would often spend the night over her house. Grandma Humphrey was very strict and did not play me spending the night out but with Starr it was different. Grandma Humphrey loved Starr and her mother so her house was one of the few places I was allowed to go. Starr is just like family and because people often commented on how much we looked alike that they automatically assumed we were related.

As I reflect back on my life, I think about everyone who had a direct impact whether it was negative or positive and I realize that I couldn't have faced this bitter sweet journey all alone. God put some angels in my life to assist me to get to my destination and it was time for me to let go of my worries, but that was easier said than done. I often think to myself – what if we knew for certain that everything we're worried about today will work out fine? What if we had a guarantee that all the problems bothering us would be worked out in the most perfect way, and at the best possible time? Or, what if we knew that a few years from now we'd be grateful for that problem, and its solution?

That week I partied and had a good time but most of all I stayed away from trouble. I went to visit my grandmother and I wanted to believe I made her my last promise. I did say I wanted to believe it would be.

The big day arrived and I had my bus ticket to leave from Greyhound bus terminal in Stamford, Connecticut. I thought I was going to be the only person heading to the center. It seemed like that bus

Job Corps

picked up a student or two at every stop. The only reason I knew this is because they were all getting sent off by someone like a social worker or probation officer...let's just say anyone other than a family member.

Some of the people that got on the bus in Bridgeport looked familiar to me but one thing for certain, they didn't look happy. Although I had a few butterflies in my stomach, I felt better than how some of those people looked because I had the opportunity to visit the center beforehand so I knew what to expect. We talked and introduced ourselves on the bus and surprisingly enough, some of the girls said they knew me, but what I think they really meant was they heard of me.

When we arrived at the center, I must say the atmosphere reminded me of an old prison movie. You know when the bus pulls up to the prison and everyone is lined up to see the "fresh meat". I checked in and was assigned a peer mentor to show me around, etc. After having all my belongings searched by security, I went to my dorm to get settled in.

I swear I wasn't in my room for more than twenty minutes before a group of girls came to my door calling my name. I opened the door and it was some of my girls from the old neighborhood and they said they heard I was coming to Job Corps that day. These girls were from all over and they were mad cool. They didn't start trouble but they were the type of girls that would have my back if I got into some trouble. They knew me and they also knew I had heart and because we were all from the old neighborhood I had their back as well. It's not like I was looking to get into trouble, but since I was miles away from home, living in a dorm with strange fe-

New Beginnings

males that I didn't know from everywhere...you know the type...those claiming to be hard...those wanting to be hard...and those that just looked hard. I just needed to be prepared for whatever.

Before dinner, I met my roommate who was from Boston. She grew up in the same neighborhood as New Edition and had all the proof to prove it which was the pollard pictures she plastered all round the room. She was very quiet and she even had a boyfriend. They were together all of the time and they looked so cute together that I believe that they got married and are living happily every after.

I met with my counselor to receive my class schedule and she told me about the different programs that are offered at the center such as job placement, driving school, etc. I haven't decided if I liked her at this point, but one thing I knew for certain...she was very loud. I remember her yelling in the hall one day "Humphrey I got my eyes on you." I wasn't sure what that meant, but it didn't take long to find out she had been in contact with my social worker. She had access to read my file, so it was only natural that she formed her opinion about me prior to my arrival.

ALL
Cookies
ain't
Sweet
A Childhood Story

CHAPTER 8
TRYING TO KEEP ON TRACK

Days, weeks and even months had passed and I have managed to remain focused and not allow myself or anyone else for that matter, take me off my path to success...in other words, I stayed out of trouble. I had goals and I was determined to follow through with each and every one of them no matter what. I am doing well in all my education classes and will soon be entering into the nursing program. To be honest, I didn't choose nursing because I wanted to become a nurse; but because it was one of the quickest programs to complete and after doing my research,

I realized there was a high demand for nursing assistants which meant it would be easier for me to secure a position that was in great demand.

Job Corps

I didn't get a chance to go home for the first month or so, but it wasn't because I wasn't welcomed, it was because I had to put my education first in my life so I chose to stay at the center for a while. I have to admit that I became somewhat homesick, but it certainly wasn't like this was the first time I was ever away from home, but it definitely was the farthest I had ever been.

My roommate and I got along fine except for one problem, she was not the tidiest person to live with and that became a huge problem for me because I'm the total opposite. At first I didn't say anything to her, but instead I chose to throw out little hints that didn't seem to work. The center was very big on student recognition and they conducted a weekly awards assembly. In addition to that, the dorms gave out certain awards and gift certificates for the best kept room. I knew that winning one of those awards would be a piece a cake for me, but a few weeks went by and we would always fail inspection because of my roommate's untidy side of the room.

I have never been a sore looser, but I refused to continue to loose out because of someone else, so I decided to have a talk with my roommate. I informed her that the reason we keep failing room inspection is because she refuse to keep her side of the room clean and that it is not my responsibility to clean the entire room but only the side that I currently occupy. Our bathroom was connected to another room so therefore we had to share it with two other girls. I truly didn't like this either because it seemed like I was the only one cleaning the bathroom. Our bathroom had a problem with the water leaking and the floor was always wet and that was another problem in itself. The following week our room was inspected and we

Trying to Keep on Track

won and we continued to win many times after that. We received gift certificates and/or movie passes. We even got a chance to go to dinner with one of the residential staff members which meant we left the center for a few hours.

I was excelling very fast through the program, and I received many awards for my efforts. One time I received seven awards in one day and it seemed like every time I went to sit down, my name was being called again. I remember one of the staff members saying I should just sit on the stage and that way I wouldn't have to walk so far. It was truly a great day and I knew I had worked really hard to receive each and every one of them awards.

My social worker was receiving great feedback from the center about my progress and she told me that she was coming for a visit and that she had a big surprise for me but wouldn't tell me what it was. Mrs. Cohen had no problem telling me when she was proud of me and when she wasn't. She has been my social worker for the past four years and we have grown to learn so much about one another. I have listened to some of the students complain about how much they hated their social worker that I feel really lucky to have mine's. Mrs. Cohen always kept her word to me and that is one of the main reasons I respected her the way that I did. She came to the center as promised and her big surprise was my Grandma Humphrey. I was so happy to see them both and I received a pass to take each of them to meet my teachers so they could see my grades, ask questions and get feedback.

For once I felt good about bringing anyone to meet my teachers. Each one had great things to say and that I was passing all my classes with a 90% aver-

Job Corps

age. My favorite teacher was my English teacher and she told both my grandmother and Mrs. Cohen that she thought I was a good writer and hoped that I would continue onto college once I graduated from the program. She also mentioned that she had recommended me to take my GED because she felt I was ready. My grandmother appeared to have a disappointed look on her face as if she wanted to hear something negative about me...or at least that's how I perceived it. I was so proud of all my awards and I couldn't wait to bring them to my room to show them off.

My grandmother came to see me because she was moving to Georgia in a few weeks and wanted to make sure I was doing alright before she left. She told me she can now leave with a piece of mind. They came around lunch time so we all had lunch together in the cafeteria. I remember Grandma Humphrey asking me if I really liked it there and I told her yes. She said she was surprised at my answer because she knew I didn't like listening or taking orders from anyone. My social worker looked at me to see how I was going to respond to her comment but all I said was "this place is different." I figured if I'm trying to change, the first step is controlling what I say and my reactions to others.

Well our first visit went really well and they both left feeling good and I felt a sense of achievement. I made copies of all my paperwork for my social worker and my grandmother to take back with them.

I had a boyfriend at the center but he just wasn't any boyfriend, he had very close ties with both my mother and father's side of the family. Neither of us knew how great our family connections were. David Davis was my Job Corp sweetheart and even though

Trying to Keep on Track

we really didn't know each other that well from the old neighborhood, our families kept us informed on how strong the family ties were. David's grandmother and Grandma Humphrey use to be next door neighbors and were good friends; my mother and his aunt were best friends; and on top of that, my Uncle Fats hung out with his uncles, so yes, you can say undeniably that there was a great deal of history between us.

David was extremely book smart and excelled in all his classes; but he was very silly as most sixteen year old boys are.

David would come to my dorm to get me to go eat in the cafeteria and walk me back to my dorm. We spent a lot of time together and he was a comedian so he kept me laughing. At some point we broke up and he started seeing this girl from Bridgeport named Tuesday. Tuesday and her Bridgeport girls were straight trouble and I had already started inquiring about them from some people on the center who was from Bridgeport. Other than David, Tuesday and I really didn't have any other explanation as to why we had become enemies...but the bottom line was we did.

I heard that Tuesday and her girls were in the recreation room talking about me and I'm not sure if David knew that it was one of his friends that came and told me. I know I should have ignored it but I didn't; I lost my temper and reacted. I went to find Tracey Rivers, Sonya Hunter, and Hope to let them know what was going on. I told them I was not going to fight, but I took my combination lock off my locker and I put on the ring that my Uncle Fats gave me just in case. I just wanted the girls there for backup in case anyone tried to jump me. We left the dorm and

Job Corps

headed straight to the recreation hall. As I was on my way in, I saw David and he said I don't know what's about to happen but Cookie don't look too happy and I think someone is getting ready to pay. So he left and went back to his dorm.

    I guess by the way we entered the recreation room one could tell something was about to happen so everyone automatically cleared the pathway from where Tuesday was standing. I walked straight up to her and said if you have something to say, just say it to my face. I don't remember what she said but it was the wrong answer. I hit her dead in the face with the lock and she hit me back and I damn near beat her half to death. I remember she was wearing extensions which were now lying on the floor. Security came and I remember passing the ring and the lock to one of my girls.

    Security then pulled the both of us aside and Tuesday was bleeding so badly that they called for an ambulance to take her to Chicopee Hospital where she stayed for some time. Needless to say, early curfew was called and everyone had to go back to their dorms. Tuesday told security that I hit her with a lock so they kept me while they searched my room to see if my lock was on my locker. What they didn't know is that I had two locks, the one they gave me, and the one I bought so when they searched my room the lock was on my locker.

    When I got back to my room my roommate asked me what had happened and I told her only what I wanted her to know. She told me she never liked Tuesday anyway. After several hours had passed, Tuesday came back but refused to stay in the same dorm with me. They put her in the honor's dorm for the night. The next morning I woke up and had truly

Trying to Keep on Track

forgotten what had happened the day before but was reminded when I walked into the cafeteria because everyone started calling me Ali.

   As usual, I went to class but by ten o'clock I was called to the administration building and I knew that wasn't good. My heart was beating so fast because there was a 90% chance that I was going to be expelled on the spot. As soon as I stepped foot inside the building, I was immediately called into the office. Once inside, I noticed Tuesday sitting there with this goofy look on her face. I immediately felt a bad vibe, but I sat down anyway. I was asked to tell my side of the story and before I could speak, I glanced down on the desk and I noticed the handful of the braids I had pulled out of Tuesday's head starring me in the face. We were both being sent home for two weeks and then we had to return back to face the review board who would then determine whether we stayed or not. Tuesday stated that she feared for her life and did not want to be on the same bus with me. She had also mentioned that there was a rumor that there would be some girls waiting to fight her when she arrived at the Greyhound bus station in Bridgeport.

   I had heard that same rumor but I wasn't the one who put it in motion. I was told that if anything happens to her during those two weeks, the center was holding me accountable and I wouldn't be allowed to come back at all. I looked Tuesday in the face and said "from what I hear, you are not well liked in Bridgeport" and I certainly can't be held responsible for that. It was more than obvious the officer was not on my side and caring only about her safety and not mines; but it was ok because I had bigger fish to fry. I was on a mission to find out who was setting her up at the bus station and ask them to reconsider. I also had

Job Corps

to come up with a hell of an explanation to tell my foster mother as to why I was coming home for two weeks.

They sent Tuesday home on the first bus and put me on the next one so that gave me ample time to find out who arranged to have her jumped. When I did, I explained to them that if anything happened to her during her two weeks at home, I was being held accountable and kicked out of the program. Sadly, Tuesday and her sister were not liked too much by many of the Bridgeport females; and my sources told me that she had a bad reputation for sleeping around. I really didn't care about that. All I cared about was her remaining safe and out of harm's way for the next two weeks.

Not long after I packed all my belongings I was dropped off at the bus station. It all happened so fast I didn't have a chance to say good bye to my roommate or any of the staff members. I had been there for approximately five months and the majority of the staff treated me very well. All the while on my ride home, I was thinking a great deal about what transpired and the steps I could have taken to prevent it. It was truly one of those moments in my life that I wish I could erase and start over with a different outcome because I had so much to loose.

I made it home safely and tried to keep what happened at the center from Wennie. I can't even recall the lie I told her as to why I came home. I had only been home a few times since I entered the program so Wennie was more interested in how I was doing. I know my social worker always kept her informed of my social and behavioral progress, so up until this point, she knew I was doing good; but I knew once

Trying to Keep on Track

she found out the truth, it was going to break her heart.

Well a week went by and all was well, and then it happened, Wennie received a phone call from the center informing her of the incident and of course she asked me numerous questions just to see if she would catch me in more lies. I did, however, tell her the truth and I remember her telling me that I better pray to God that they let me stay and you better believe I was.

ALL Cookies ain't *Sweet*

A Childhood Story

CHAPTER 9
FACING THE BOARD

I went back to the center the day before my hearing and I was welcomed back with so much love. I was happy to see my roommate and the rest of my friends. Mr. Lee was one of the first staff members that I seen upon my return and he was a very religious man. We would frequently have conversations regarding faith and prayer. He told me he had heard about what happened and he also told me to keep the faith and pray on it. He also suggested that I go to the education building and ask all my teachers for a recommendation letter and he would present them to the Board on my behalf.

All of my teachers knew that I haven't been in any trouble since I've been at the center until now, so they had no problem providing me with a recommendation letter. I wasn't sure what the end result

Job Corps

would be, so I didn't come back to the center with all my belongings just in case they decided to terminate me.

I went back to my room pretending everything was fine with me when really, it wasn't. In less than forty-eight hours, people who didn't know me were going to determine whether I should stay in the program or be terminated. I know some people who went before the Board and got terminated, left the same day and never returned. My roommate kept telling me not to worry because it may not be as bad as I think it is. I asked her if she ever faced the Board before and she said no; but what she didn't tell me was that she was sitting on the Board and that's why she didn't want me to worry because I wasn't leaving the center.

I couldn't wait for morning so I could get it over and done with. Tuesday had her appointment first and we were all waiting outside to find out if she was staying or leaving. She was in there for about an hour and I wasn't sure if that was a good or bad thing, but when she came out, she had a silly smile on her face and her friends were cheering. This was the first time I have ever seen the center divided like it was. More than half of the center, including staff and students, were all on my side and there was talk about starting a riot if I get terminated.

My appointment was scheduled for two o'clock and no one wanted to leave the court yard until I came back. I have always been the one who is on time, so I arrived approximately ten minutes early. The door was closed so I had to wait out in the hall. The door opened up a few minutes before two and I was asked to step inside. When I entered the room, there sat my English teacher who I adored, Mr. Lee and my

Facing the Board

roommate. I remember my roommate looking directly at me and winking her eye and my English teacher gave me a big smile.

They explained what was going to take place and everyone around the table introduced themselves. I was then asked to explain the incident with Tuesday. I was asked some questions by the Board and each person at the table said something positive about me and expressed why they thought I should stay. When I spoke I also apologized for my part in what happened and stated why I believe I should remain at the center. I have been representing myself for quite some time so of course that part came natural to me. I spoke very clear and my message came across as being sincere.

I was asked to step out of the room so that they could complete the ruling process which took less than five minutes. In that short period of time, I must have paced the floor several times. When the door finally opened, I was asked to step back inside. Needless to say, the Board voted for me to stay and I was given a verbal warning. What this meant is that I cannot get into any more trouble during the rest of my duration in the program.

I thanked each Board member and I left with a big smile on my face and a huge sense of relief. It seemed like the entire center was waiting outside and so was Tuesday and her crew. I guess she just knew I was going home but God spared me once again.

I started walking fast towards my room and they were yelling out did I get terminated. I wanted to say yes, but then I remembered that they threatened to riot so I didn't say a word. I just wanted to get back to my room so I could call Wennie and my social worker

Job Corps

to tell them the good news, so I yelled back that I didn't get terminated and I will be around until I graduate in three months.

I am now ready to put this all behind me and move forward with a new attitude. I completed all my educational classes and was ready to take my GED. From what I heard the test was very difficult because they take twelve years of education and crammed it into a four hour test. I took the test and had to wait a few weeks for my results to come back and when they finally arrived, I had passed everything except the math section which was no surprise to me because math was not one of my strongest subjects.

The good thing about it was I didn't have to retake the entire test, just the math portion. I had taken the math part twice and failed, but I was determined not to leave the program without passing this part of the test. I'm sure you are familiar with the phrase "the third time is a charm" because I finally passed the math portion of the test and received my GED.

This was a two-year program which can be completed earlier depending on what you wanted and/or needed. I needed my GED/diploma because I wanted a quick trade so I can go to work immediately. After graduating, my goal was to work full-time for the first two years. I have only three and a half more months to go before I complete the program and the only thing I had left to do now was to complete my trade and my intern and that was all based on hours. Of course, the longer you stayed in the program, the more money you will earn. But, I felt I could double the money once I graduated and started working.

It was time to say goodbye to my roommate who was graduating in a few weeks. I believe she had

Facing the Board

been there for over a year. I'm not sure if she was going back to Boston or not, but I do recall her having a little daughter. My roommate was very quiet and spent the majority of her time with her now fiancée...yes, she got engaged to her boyfriend despite all the pain she had experienced in her life.

Even though I was going to miss her, the chance to have the entire room to myself was a great feeling, even if it meant that would only last for a few weeks or so. After she left, one of the dorm staff (RA) told me that due to the water problems in the bathroom, they will not be assigning me another roommate. She also told me that I was next on the list to move into the honor's dorm which was a co-ed dorm for students who are academically and socially excelling. The rooms were much bigger and nicer than the one I occupied and the students receive additional privileges. But as good as it all sounds, I declined, I wanted and needed my own privacy and space and that meant more to me than moving to a nicer room.

I am and will always be a critical thinker and my thought process is not like most. In order for me to concentrate, I need my own space with total peace and quiet. For those reasons alone, I continued the remainder of my stay in room 216 which just so happens to have been my Grandma Humphrey's house number for the past twenty-one years.

ALL Cookies ain't *Sweet*

A Childhood Story

CHAPTER 10
MY GRADUATION CELEBRATION

I have received my letter from Job Corps that stated I have met all the necessary requirements to graduate and I have been offered a job at a municipal state hospital in Springfield, MA. I dreamt about this day and it finally came. I can't believe I was willing to throw my future away over something so stupid...which was my pride. I was extremely proud of all my accomplishment I achieved at Westover Job Corps Center.

For once in my life, I followed through with making the necessary adjustments in order for me to complete school, my attitude improved, and now I am focused on my career. I knew being a nursing aid was not my career choice, but I enjoyed interacting and assisting other people. Besides that, I also needed

Job Corps

more time to figure out which direction in life I really wanted to go.

Because I had a job lined up in Springfield which is about twenty minutes away from Chicopee, I decided to stay in Massachusetts and find an apartment close to the hospital. I started working with the apartment counselor who helped students find affordable housing prior to leaving the center. However, Job Corps didn't give out stipends until you have officially left and they have verified your employment, etc. Before leaving the center, I was told when to return for the graduation ceremony.

I decided to go home for a few weeks and hang out with some of my friends and family, but after a week of that, I was ready to head back to Massachusetts. At this point in my life, I knew I had changed; I wasn't the same Cookie that they knew. Within those eight and a half months I had matured and was no longer interested in doing the things I use to. Thanks to Job Corps, I found a new sense of independence and I have to say, it felt good.

I headed back a week earlier and stayed with an RA who worked at the Job Corp center. I wasn't scheduled to report to my new job for another month, so I started looking for an apartment on my own. When I last spoke to Grandma Humphrey, she told me she bought her airline ticket and was looking forward to attending my graduation and then a few days prior to graduation; she called to say she was sick and will be unable to attend. I was disappointed to hear this because she was the one person I really wanted to see. I am not sure why my foster mother and social worker didn't show, but the truth is, none of my friends or family members were there. I felt so alone and was very hurt. I felt like it was one of the biggest days of my life

My Graduation Celebration

and I had no one to share it with. But I had the Job Corp staff there for me and they were the ones who were working and even the ones that were off duty attended the graduation ceremony.

Of course I had my favorite residential aid and teachers and they had their favorite students. My favorite RA's was Ms. Hazel because she didn't play at all. Then there was Ms. Ellison, and Mrs. Franklin. Ms. Ellison helped me put on my cap and gown and then took pictures of me. She could tell something was bothering me so I told her that my grandmother wasn't able to make it because she was sick.

Ms. Ellison said that this day was about me and I needed to focus on that instead so I did. As I marched with my class and as my name was being called, I had a slight flashback of my life. I thought about everything that took place prior to me stepping on that stage to receive my diploma and that's when it happened...the tears of joy, sorrow and pain started to fall. My bitter sweet was finally starting to taste good.

The ceremony was very nice and I walked away with some additional awards and certificates. I took pictures with a lot of my friends, signed autograph books and went around the center saying my final goodbyes.

Westover Job Corps gave me a new start on life...actually it saved my life. I was provided with the structure and the tools I needed to succeed and the solid foundation to build on. It's a wonderful program and I will forever be grateful for the experience.

Job Corps

Me and Kim chillin' on the Job Corps float.

Job Corp is the nation's largest and most comprehensive residential education and job training program for at-risk youth, ages 16 through 24. Job Corps combines classroom, practical, and work-based learning experiences to prepare youth for stable, long-term, high-paying jobs.

There are 122 Job Corps centers located throughout the United States, each offering educational training and a variety of vocational training programs.

Job Corps is administered by the Department of Labor's Office of the Secretary.

Me and the crew at Virginia Beach.

Me, Paula, Fern, and Jennifer at Uncle Dave's Place.

Me at Westover Job Corps in deep thought.

Me, Fern, Paula, and Fulika having a day of fun at Six Flags.

SECTION 3
MOVING ON

ALL Cookies ain't Sweet

A Childhood Story

CHAPTER 11
LIFE AFTER JOB CORPS

M oving on to bigger and better things was the next phase of my life. After graduation, I went to stay with Mrs. Franklin temporarily. I was only expected to be there until I found an apartment, but I stayed there for approximately five months.

I had to keep my staying with Mrs. Franklin a secret because that was against Job Corps' policy, especially with her still working there. I don't believe she would have gotten in that much trouble because I was no longer a resident. Mrs. Franklin knew I was offered the job at the hospital and in fact, it was about a fifteen minute walk from her house so she said until I move into my apartment, I was welcomed to stay with her.

Mrs. Franklin had a daughter name Janet who was a year or so older than me. Janet was happy to show

Moving On

me around the city and she even introduced me to some of her friends and family. However, we were definitely two different types of people and sometimes we would bump heads. Mr. Franklin was very nice too. He worked hard and stayed to himself mostly. It was clear that Janet was a daddy's girl and the two of them were very close but the relationship she had with her mother wasn't all that good.

It's funny because no matter how much you think you know someone, you really don't. At work Mrs. Franklin was extremely nice and appeared to be very professional; but during my short stay at her home, I learned that she is a drug addict. I'm not talking weed or cocaine; I'm talking about drugs that don't bring you home for days and weeks at a time.

I would often hear Mrs. Franklin and her husband arguing about it and she and Janet would even fight about it. Once I started working, I was very careful with how I spent my money. Along with Mrs. Franklin's drug addiction other habits and bad behavior started to surface. But once I started putting in some overtime, I wasn't around the house that much. I worked every other weekend and the weekends I had off, I went to Connecticut or New York.

I really liked my new state job and the benefits were good too. At the hospital is where the name Cassondra was given to me because on my floor there were two other nurses aids named Sandra, so one of my co-workers said she was going to call me Cassondra, because I pronounced "Sandra" with an "o",. I never gave it a second thought and that name has followed me ever since. Although it doesn't bother me when people call me ether, I prefer Cookie. My birth name "Sandra Gail Humphrey" was

Life after Job Corps

given to me by my father's sister (Aunt Sandy) who I was named after.

I worked second shift which was from three to eleven but because I was seventeen, I was required by law to be off the street at ten o'clock. I didn't necessarily care for that shift because I didn't know how to drive nor did I have a car. Even though this wasn't my first job, I did consider it my first real job and every Thursday was payday. I opened up an account with their credit union and the majority of my check went directly into my savings for my apartment. I would pay the Franklins every week for allowing me to stay there but when I would give the money to Mrs. Franklin, one can only imagine what she did with it so Mr. Franklin asked me not give any more money to her so I started giving it to him.

Mrs. Franklin had a friend who was a nurse that she would sometimes hang out with, but by the looks of her, I could tell she was up to no good. She was known for making strange gestures and fidgeting a lot. Well after I had been at the hospital for about five months, guess who else started working there...Ms. Franklin's friend. She started off doing quite well and then it happened, patient's medications started mysteriously disappearing and she was constantly calling off work. Shortly thereafter, the gossip about her possibly being an addict started circulating and eventually she lost her job in a matter of months.

I rarely went to the credit union (because it was too far) to withdraw money out of my account, but somehow Mrs. Franklin got a hold of my bank information and tried to withdraw a large sum of money from my account. However, she couldn't provide them with the correct account number so she didn't receive any funds so they flagged my account.

Moving On

About a month later my co-worker Linda asked me to ride with her to the credit union during lunch break and I did. While I was there, I decided to take out some money but when I gave the teller my withdrawal slip, she gave me this strange look and directed me to a booth and told me that someone will assist me. Of course I didn't think anything was wrong because all this was new to me. The teller came out and asked me to show her my identification and by then, my co-worker came over to see what was going on. The teller explained that someone came in a few weeks earlier posing as me and tried to withdraw money out of my account. I explained that I was new to the city and didn't know too many people so I wasn't sure who that might have been. But for some strange reason, Mrs. Franklin's name popped up in my head and I asked the teller to please describe the person to me. She did better than that, she showed me a picture that was taken and it had the time and date on it. To my surprise, it was Mrs. Franklin and right then and there I knew I had no choice but to take my apartment search more seriously.

Linda was more upset about what happened than I was. She knew that Mrs. Franklin was taking advantage of me. Linda asked me if I was going to confront her and I told her that it wouldn't do me any good because Mrs. Franklin is a drug addict and she would not tell me the truth. By this time, I had saved over three thousand dollars and I had eleven hundred left from my Job Corp stipend. But after adding up all the apartment expenses, I knew I had to hang in there just a little while longer and save up some more money. All my co-workers were very helpful because on their days off and even on the weekends,

Life after Job Corps

they each would take turns taking me around to look at apartments.

Because I had been working long hours, I haven't had a chance to speak to my social worker so I decided to give her a call. We talked for a good while and I was telling her about some of my elderly patients and how fun some of them are. She expressed how proud she was of the new person I had become and how I turned my life around. I told her that I was looking for an apartment and she said once I get one; the State would be able to assist me. She further explained a program called "transitional living" and what this program does is help young people, like me, who are living independently on their own and are working and/or going to school. In addition, she mentioned how the State could help me purchase furniture and things of that nature. Lastly, she said she would send me an information packet to read over along with an application for me to fill out and send back to her.

Although I never said a word to Mrs. Franklin about my knowing what she tried to do, my attitude towards her changed drastically. She went from being someone I trusted and often spoke with, to someone who I couldn't trust and didn't want to hold any conversations with at all. The old Cookie would have jumped on her, but the new Cookie put the problem in God's hands for handling, so I chose to pray for her instead. It makes me wonder if this was her plan from the very beginning and was that the reason why she offered me to stay with her.

One Friday I decided to go home for the weekend because there were some things I needed to take care of so I took some money out the bank. I realized that I had about three hundred and fifty dollars

Moving On

more than I needed so I ask Mr. Franklin to put it up for me until I return home. I told him he was welcome to use any of it if he needed to. He thanked me and then he put it inside the Bible upstairs in the attic. He showed me where he put it and said it will be there when I got back. As far as I know, no one else was in the house except the two of us at the time, so I went outside to wait for my cab.

I went home for the weekend and spent some time with my family and friends; it was one of those quick but sweet mini vacations. When I got back it was late Sunday and after settling in, I went up in the attic to get my money only it wasn't there. Mr. Franklin wasn't home so I figured he probably moved it, so I waited for him to come home and I asked him for it. He said it was in the Bible where he left it. I asked him to come and show me where he put it and sure enough my money was gone. Mr. Franklin stated the only person in the house crazy enough to steal out of a Bible would be his wife and she hasn't been seen in a couple of days. I thought to myself she stole my money and was somewhere getting high.

One of my co-workers told me about a vacancy in her building for a studio apartment. She explained the apartment setup which seemed perfect for me and it was on the first floor. She had already spoken with the landlord and told me to give him a call so he could show me the apartment. The next day I went home with my co-worker and I waited at her house until the landlord came. She told me that the setup downstairs was the same which had an eat-in kitchen which was small, a bathroom and one mid-size room with two closets. She lived with her boyfriend and together they had a lot of stuff so it looked a little over crowded.

Life after Job Corps

The landlord came and he showed me the apartment. I instantly fell in love with it and asked when I could move in. He said I had to first fill out a credit application and pay the thirty dollar fee along with the security deposit. He also said he had to conduct a credit check and once everything came back fine, I could come to the office and sign the lease and pick up my keys.

My co-worker was with me and asked a lot of important questions that I didn't think to ask. She knew this was my first apartment so her being there helped out tremendously. She said she would take me to his office so I would know where it is if I ever had to go there again. The landlord called and said I got approved for the apartment so we set up a time that I could come and sign my lease and pick up the keys to my very first apartment. My rent was only two hundred eighty dollars, so I paid my rent for the three months in advance. I informed the Franklins that I got approved for an apartment and would be moving out in a few weeks.

I called my social worker the next day to tell her the good news and to find out about the next steps on receiving my monthly stipend. She said she would have to come to Springfield to make sure that the apartment was safe and fit for me to live in. She said this was standard state procedure and part of the process so not to worry. My social worker came on my day off with another social worker who was in training. They brought me a nice gift basket with towels, sheets, pots, pans, etc. She said she bought the house warming gift herself because she didn't know how long it would take for the paperwork to be processed and she didn't want me to be without. They really liked the apartment and the idea that the police sta-

Moving On

tion was just up the street. She said she would have no problem signing off on the paperwork. We went out for a quick lunch and then we went by the hospital so she could see where I worked. They couldn't stay long because they had to go to Job Corps to visit another client. I was glad to see her and she was glad to see me too.

Wow, it's hard to believe that the year has come and gone. I'm eighteen now and according to the state that makes me somewhat legal, well at least legal enough for them to stop my stipend for a few months, but my social worker said once I turned eighteen it was going to end because I was working full-time and was considered self sufficient. She also informed me that she was going to be retiring and moving to Israel which was her hometown. That came as a shock to me and I was saddened by the news but happy for her at the same time, because she has been a part of my life for so many years and I really liked her.

It took me less than two months to furnish my studio apartment and it was perfect. Wennie (my foster mother) also gave me a lot of towels, sheets, pots and pans and even curtains, so I had everything I needed. I came from a long line of cooks starting with Grandma Humphrey and all her sisters and brothers and Wennie too, but because I worked sixteen-hour days, I mostly ate fast food and spent very little time in the kitchen.

For once, I finally felt a sense of freedom and security. I was happy for more than a few hours out of a day and I felt free inside. It's hard for me to explain or put into words, but I finally had a sense of inner peace...yeah that's it...inner peace...kind of like the calm before the storm. I was growing up and taking

Life after Job Corps

responsibility for my actions, while making decisions that would have an impact on my daily life.

For a brief moment, I remember being upset with God. I began to question whether He really exist because I had a hard time believing that someone with so much love and power would allow so many bad things to happen to me at such a young age. But the more I learned about myself the better I understood God, His mission and His purpose in my life. I grew up attending church, so God was no stranger to me, but I still wasn't sure what He wanted from me. It almost seemed like I was His target and He was aiming straight for my heart and I basically needed help to understand why.

ALL Cookies ain't *Sweet*

A Childhood Story

CHAPTER 12

MOVING FORWARD

Life for me was going great and even though I was working very hard to support myself and maintain my financial obligations, I was also taking in the sites and attractions which Springfield had to offer. I had stayed in touch with one of my friends from Job Corps, Sara Hunt who lives in Hartford, CT and we would take turns spending the night at each other's place. Sara still lived at home so she looked forward to coming to Springfield to hang out with me. We had so much in common. We both were born under the Aquarius sign and our birthdays were two days apart. In addition to us sharing the same style of fashion, it would be nothing for us to get dressed and pull out the same outfit just in different colors. On this particular Saturday, not only did we pull out the same

Moving On

outfit, but it was the same color and we bought it in two different states.

I believe Sara was maybe a year or two older than me, but one thing is certain, neither one of us was twenty-one. There was this hot nightclub called Profiles in Springfield where a lot of people went to party; and even though I wasn't twenty-one, I had no problems getting through the front door because one of my co-workers worked there. Sara and I went to the club and were having a good time. She saw a lot of people she knew from Hartford. She saw her friend Smitty who introduced me to his friend Anthony Moore.

Anthony was with his cousin and friend and Smitty introduced everyone. Anthony asked what Sara and I were drinking and bought us a couple of long island ice teas. At this point, there were three guys, Anthony, his cousin and his friend sitting with Sara and me. Anthony's friend started talking to Sara and Anthony and I started talking so that left his cousin out the loop so he was ready to leave. Anthony was driving so he asked what we were doing after the club and I told him that Sara was staying the night and we were going back to my place. I told him we were walking so he said he would drop his cousin off and come right back to hang out with us.

We waited for a while for the guys after the club was over, but we didn't see them so just when we decided to start walking home they pulled up and gave us a ride. They came in and stayed for a while. That was the first time I ever had more than three people in my apartment at one time. Anthony and I were talking about the typical stuff like did we have a boy/girlfriend or did we have any children and he seemed cool so we exchanged phone numbers.

Life after Job Corps

Sara liked his friend so they exchanged pager numbers. The following day Anthony and his friend came by the house so he could say goodbye to Sara before she left to go home. I guess they planned this because Anthony let his friend drive Sara home and he stayed behind with me until he got back.

Anthony and I started spending a lot of time together after that day. Although we had a lot in common, we also realized we had our differences. I'm talking Bobby Brown and Whitney Houston different. But as the saying goes "opposites attract" and we did. He could tell that I was different from most girls he dated in the past. At eighteen, I was employed full-time, had my own place, no children and I had goals and ambition. We started out pretty good...so I thought. I was still new to the area so this was a great advantage for him, not to mention that I worked the eleven to seven shifts. It didn't take me long to find out that he was living the fast life and spent most of his time in the streets and on the block. We both liked nice things, but our views on how to get them were very different.

Anthony's nickname is "Ant Rock" and once I added that to his street credentials I was able to figure out his true hustle. But by that time, I was already in love with him and found it harder to walk away, so I chose to ignore what he was doing and stayed with him. Besides, it wasn't like I didn't reap the benefits of being his girlfriend. I was always showered with expensive gifts and we took lavish trips. Even though Anthony told me when we first met that he didn't have any children, one of my co-workers who lived next door to his mother, made a comment about how much his daughter resembled him. I remember asking what daughter? I said we can't be talking about the

Moving On

same person because the Anthony I am speaking of has no children. I thought to myself why would someone lie about having a child. I remember thinking to myself Lord what have I got myself into.

Shortly after that Anthony introduced me to his family. He lived with his grandparents Mr. and Mrs. Jennings. Both appeared to be very nice but there was something about his grandfather that I just loved. He was so caring and acted as if he had no problems in the world. Anthony was the only boy but he has an older sister who both shared the same father and two younger sisters who shared the same father. Anthony's mother also appeared to be pleasant. Although he never spoke much about his father, he did tell me that his father lived in Tennessee and he doesn't get to see him much.

Eventually, I met his daughter, who not only was beautiful, but she looked just like him. I believe she was about a year old or close to it, but she was walking and talking. I instantly fell in love with her, and she would often come over to spend the night. I love children and I missed being around all my little cousins, so she was a joy to have around and so well behaved.

I had told Anthony early on that I was an only child however, I was raised by my foster mother and I have two sisters and a brother. Anthony would soon enough meet some of my family, Wennie, Fern, Paula, Danny and my cousin Alan. The first time Wennie met him, she told me to get rid of him because people who are that quiet are sneaky and are always up to no damn good. Again...another warning sign that I ignored.

Before I started seriously seeing Anthony, I was studying to be a flight attendant. As much as I loved

Life after Job Corps

children, I didn't want to have any because I wasn't sure if I was the mothering type. Even though I knew I would never leave my child, I just wasn't sure if I would be a good mother. I don't think he liked the idea of me becoming a flight attendant because that meant that I would be gone most of the time and we would not be seeing much of each other, so I eventually gave that up.

The more time we spent together, the more I got to learn who he really was, and the more disappointed I became. He was a typical eighteen year old male trying to live his life, do him and have his cake and eat it too. I, on the other hand, knew what I wanted and where I was trying to go in life. I wanted to be loved, so of course once he said he loved me, I had thought that I found love. Although we were both young, I was mentally more mature than he was.

Anthony and I celebrated our first year together and I must admit the time passed rather quickly. I was unclear as to where our relationship was headed and would often ask him about it. Our relationship started to take a turn between me working all the time and him just never making time, I became unhappy and I could tell he sensed that so we decided to take a vacation together.

He booked us a five day, four night trip to Freeport, Bahamas. Neither one of us had ever left the United States before, so it was a great experience for the both of us. I had a wonderful time and this was the first time, since we have been together, that I actually seen him relax.

Moving On

Me and Anthony enjoying Bahamas Blue Sky.

Me and Anthony on vacation in Freeport.

Moving Forward

We took in the sun, the beach and the night life. I wasn't much of a gambler, but I played the slot machines and watched him tear the black jack table up winning each time.

We enjoyed our time together and he really made me feel very special. We talked about the past, as well as the future and I really felt that he meant the things that he was saying about changing his life style. It all sounded so good but almost too good to be true. By now he had me all figured out and knew those were all the things I wanted to hear from him. Deep inside, I'm sure he wanted to change, but because he had also lacked strong guidance, he was unsure which direction to turn. Communication wasn't one of his strong areas and that was the main ingredient missing in our relationship. Communicating always came easy for me and maybe that's because it was my only means of being heard. I just couldn't understand why he had such a hard time expressing himself to me.

Well, it was the last day of our trip and we got up early to do some shopping for gifts and souvenirs. Our luggage was already packed, we had brunch and our next stop was to the airport. Neither one of us was ready to leave, but I had to get back to work. The week went by so quickly and because we were having such a great time, I wasn't ready for it all to end. But somehow I knew things would go back to normal once we got back home.

Things seemed to be going fine with us for a few weeks or so, but physically I wasn't feeling so good. I started feeling very sick to my stomach and I was vomiting a lot. Anthony started to sleep a lot which was rare for him so he mentioned to me that he thought I might be pregnant and wanted me to go to

Moving On

the doctor. I was in denial, so therefore I put off going to see the doctor for a few weeks. We both went together and he waited in the car. I took the standard urine test which came back positive. I remember the doctor telling me those exact words "it's positive" and based on my last period I was about six weeks along. I was stunned, happy but yet sad at the same time, because I always said I never wanted to have children in fear that I may not be a good mother. Once my appointment was over, I headed back to the car and Anthony asked me what did the doctor say? I said the doctor said I was about six weeks pregnant and he smiled. I knew he would be very happy because he wanted me to have a baby with him. I was in love with him so of course I wanted to make him happy but the truth is...we were both only nineteen. Besides, he already had a two year old daughter from a previous relationship, so I felt the timing wasn't exactly right for us.

Well the news got back to my family and friends that I was pregnant and was going to have Anthony's baby. But there was a rumor going around that he had gotten another girl pregnant and she was keeping the baby. At the time, I didn't know who the person was, but I asked him about the rumor and he said it wasn't true. For this to only be an alleged rumor; it became the talk of the town and I had no choice but to believe it. So I did some investigating and was able to provide him with names and enough information which got his attention and even though he still denied it, I didn't believe him so I left him.

Its painful finding out that you've been cheated on, but what was more disturbing was that he would risk my health and our relationship for some round the way chick with a salty reputation. I felt betrayed and

Moving Forward

had lost all respect for him. Not only was I a faithful girlfriend to him, I never compromised our health. It was all starting to make sense to me now, all that we needed to take a vacation crap was only to prepare me for the baby boom which would eventually take place, and the romance was to help plant the right baby seed.

The girl had given birth to a baby boy a few months or two before I did and Anthony instantly denied the baby; and from what little I know, he didn't have or want much to do with her or the baby. The rumor was she was unsure who the child's father was, I almost felt bad for her because that's not a healthy or attractive situation to be in. The difference between her and I was, I knew who had fathered my child and I would never put myself in a situation where DNA is the subject surrounding my baby. He wasn't denying me or my baby, so I didn't have to deal with that.

I eventually, left Springfield and moved back home with my foster mother and family. I was seven and a half months along and facing many complications with my pregnancy and was scared to death so I was happy to be home with her so she could help me get through the child birth. I know they say one shouldn't wish for a boy or girl but ask God for the delivery of a healthy baby instead. Not only did I ask God for a healthy baby, but I asked Him for a healthy baby boy. I even went out and bought boy clothes because I just knew I was carrying a boy. I figured boys were a lot easier to raise than girls and if there was something I didn't know or needed to know I could ask Anthony.

The doctor gave me a due date of July 4th. Paula stayed with me throughout the entire delivery and

Moving On

when the baby was coming out she said "oh my God, it's a boy with a lot of hair" and I was so relieved until the doctor yelled out "it's a girl" and I was in a bit of a shock. Talk about be careful what you wish for. My bundle of joy arrived around eight o'clock that night on

July 8, 1990. I had already chosen two names, *(Semaj)*, which is actually James, spelled backwards. Anthony's first name is James so I wanted to be creative and I also liked Shanya, but for some reason, once I looked at her I didn't feel that ether of those names suited her so I named her *Breona Wennette Moore* instead. I named her Wennette after my foster mother Wennie. Wennies, real name is Wenneth, and I wanted Breona's name to have true history and meaning behind it.

Paula called Anthony to inform him that I went into labor. He was almost two hours away so by the time he got to the hospital, Breona was already born. He took one look at her and smiled. It was kind of difficult to tell who she looked like because of her chingy eyes. She kind of resembled an Asian baby, but I didn't care because I knew she was mines. I had given her my last name Humphrey which Anthony was not happy about and he wanted her last name changed to Moore as soon as possible. So that following Tuesday he came back down to sign the papers. I stayed home for a few months and Anthony and I decided to try and to work things out so I went back to Springfield and we tried to move forward together as a family. Things were going good, I went back to work and Breona was going to the daycare.

At this point, I was only trying to make it work for Breona's sake. I felt that she didn't ask to be born and the least I can do is try to make a happy home for

Moving Forward

her. I still loved Anthony, but I was no longer in love with him and I still didn't trust him not one bit. It didn't take long for him to slip back into his old ways. We soon started arguing and bickering frequently over the same old issues and one day he said things between us wasn't working out and he asked me to leave, but told me Breona could stay.

I guess you can say Anthony was the bread winner in the family, and even though I often worked two jobs it couldn't add up to his cash flow. By him asking me to leave was the first step in me seeking my independence back. Here I am with a two year old baby, very little money, and no car. I could have stayed with a friend, but with a baby, that would not be the best decision to make. I really didn't want to go back home so the next day I called a few shelters and found one that would take me that day. The only problem was the shelter was in Holyoke which was outside of Springfield. I packed what I could and put the rest in storage.

I got a friend to take me out to Holyoke and during the ride there I was praying that the shelter wasn't a dump and I kept telling myself this would only be temporary. I asked my friend to wait while I make sure everything was okay and it was so I stayed. My friend was really one of Anthony's homeboys, and I knew he liked me but because he was one of his closest friends I made sure I kept it that way.

He was around Anthony all the time and was aware of everything that was going on, and even though he never told me much, I could tell he wanted too. He would often say how lucky Anthony was and that he didn't know how good he had it and how he wishes he was in his shoes. I know he respected me because he knew that despite all the dirt

Moving On

that Anthony was doing to me, I was not out to get revenge on him. I told him that I had a daughter to raise and wanted to set a good example for her. He helped me get my things into the house and told me to call him if I need anything. I didn't want anyone to know where I was and it wasn't because I was embarrassed to be living in a shelter, but because Anthony allowed us to be there and did nothing to change that. He could have offered to leave and allowed me and the baby to stay or he could have given me time to find a suitable place for us to live and helped out with the expenses but instead, in so many words, he said make your on way...not my problem.

I am a survivor so therefore I ate those silent words and kept it moving. I have always been good with reading in between the lines and his words came across very clear. I stayed in the shelter for about three months and continued to work. I paid one of the girls who I befriended there to watch Breona for me while I was at work. During my stay in the shelter, I saved every penny I could and was searching for an apartment. The environment was very different for Breona and I hated that I had to subject her to it, but I was determined not to move back home so I did what I had to do. After a few days, I called Anthony and informed him where I was. He apologized and said he was sorry for what he did and wanted us to come back to live with him. But by now, those apologizes had gotten real old and stale. As good as it all sounded, it still wasn't good enough and I knew Breona and I deserved better. I had to search deep inside to find the person I was before I met him. Somehow I had lost focus and was depending on

Moving Forward

someone else which will never happen again. Until Breona came it was just me, myself and I.

I told him that it was okay and that Breona and I were going to stay put. The shelter was nice and clean and they assisted single young mothers and since I met the criteria, I was getting the assistance I needed at no cost. Even though a part of me wanted to go back, I stood my ground...I knew I had to break away. I guess you can say I was fed up with the games and the on and off again relationship that I knew wasn't good for either of us or our daughter. Somehow I felt bad for her because she was a daddy's girl and for a brief moment, I felt like I failed her by not keeping our family together; but I finally realized I am only one person and it takes the commitment of both parents to make not only a happy home, but a healthy relationship and family. Breona would often cry for Anthony or say "I don't want to stay here take me to my daddy". It broke my heart but it was because of Anthony that we were living there in the first place.

I didn't even let my friends or family know where I was. I just toughed it out and in the end, I got an apartment in Springfield. I had taken some driving lessons and later received my driver's license. I purchased a Dodge Horizon that later broke down on me. Anthony was trying everything to get me to come back home and I knew this because he would often buy me big gifts. His making expensive purchases meant one or two things and that is either he has done something wrong and bought a guilt gift or that he was trying to apologize for something he's done and want to make up. In this case it was a car, and it was beautiful. He put a big red bow on it and parked it in his grandfather's driveway.

Moving On

The car had been there for a while because I really didn't want to accept it. Anthony was good for giving me gifts and then taking them back, but I really needed a reliable car so I finally broke down and accepted it. I had my own place and he has his own place and this seemed to work out so much better. I started dating and I'm sure he never stopped. Even though I have accepted we were no longer a couple, he is still my daughter's father. Once I let go, I started living my life and having fun again. The sad part about it is I feel that I wasted so much time in a dead-end relationship. We were together off and on for seven years and the best part of us was Breona. I am not saying that we didn't have good times together; it's just that the bad far outweighed the good.

Around 1995 something happen which would change everyone's life. Anthony got hit with a drug charge that would send him away for seven and a half years. This was a rough time for everyone. He and I were pretty much over prior to this happening and even though I was seeing someone in New Haven, Connecticut. I hated the fact that he was caught up in this triangle. Anthony had a unique style and swagger which separated him from many in his hometown of Springfield, MA, and for those reasons, among others, there were a lot of jealous people waiting to watch him fall on his face.

Nevertheless, he went upstate to serve his time. I was now left all alone to raise Breona which was something that I was already doing, but financially Anthony was taking care of her. Breona was attending kindergarten at Sacred Heart Catholic School and taking dance lessons and she was doing great. Breona was a bit young to understand what was happening with her father and why he moved so far

Moving Forward

away. I had only been a mother for five years and I must admit was pretty damn good at it. There is no instruction book written on how to console your child to adapt to this type of situation so I turned to God and started going back to church.

Again, I started to have mixed feelings about people coming in and out of my life, but I was wondering if God removed him permentaly because He knew he wasn't the man for me. Maybe God felt that I was taken to long to figure it out on my own. It seemed like this was my chance to break free, but somehow I wasn't pleased with the outcome or the circumstances. Anthony was still Breona's father and I knew that would never change and for the first five years of her life they were inseparable.

ALL Cookies ain't *Sweet*

A Childhood Story

CHAPTER 13
Love, Baby and Life

After Anthony left I started questioning my purpose for living and staying in Springfield. I had lived in Massachusetts since 1987 and it was 1995, so about nine years. This was the longest that I had ever lived any where at one time. Breona was getting older and her needs were getting greater. She was attending private school, taking dance lessons and was being introduced to modeling which all took money. So I decided to go back to school. I knew I liked helping people but I wasn't sure in what field. I grew up around Heavy D & the Boyz and Al B. Sure so music, dancing, singing and writing was all part of the entertainment world that I wanted to explore. As I started researching my career path, I wasn't sure if the entertainment field was going to put an instant paycheck in my hands. I know if I didn't have Breona

Moving On

it would have been the road I would have chosen, but because of her, I needed something which was stable and solid.

Springfield had a lot of colleges that I could choose from, but I had to also think about the hours because I needed to work and be able to afford childcare while I attended school. Springfield College offered a great weekend Bachelor of Science program which allowed me to attend school on the weekends and receive a four-year degree in Human Services in less the time. Babysitting for me was a challenge because it was the weekend and for most people, that was their free time to do what they wanted to do or didn't have time to do during the work week. Breona was a very good girl, so many of my girlfriends had no problem keeping her for me.

Once Anthony left, I didn't hear much from his family, so I turned to my best friend Anita Smith-Lee's parents, Mr. and Mrs. Smith for support. They often kept Breona and included us in their family functions, etc. Over the years spent in Springfield, I had met some very nice people who treated Breona as if she was their very own grandchild and me as one of their children. That's how I know there are so many good people in the world and they don't have to share the same blood type as you; they just need to be human and have a heart. Breona and I were fortunate to have met such wonderful people. Anita Smith-Lee and I met through our children attending the same daycare facility. Robin Lee is Anita's daughter and because of our girls, we have become not only good friends, but Anita is Breona's Godmother and I became Robin's. Anita's parents, Mr. and Mrs. Smith, are the two most beautiful people you would ever want

Love, Baby and Life

to meet and they became my away from home parents.

Ms. Barbara Ellison is my daughter's other Godmother, who was my residential dorm aid at Job Corps. Barbara is another wonderful person with a beautiful spirit. She has a creative touch with the youths and has made a solid career providing motivation and leadership throughout the Job Corps system. Barbara directed me through some tough times and showered my daughter with so much love.

My girlfriend Christy Woods is also another dear friend. Christy was always a positive role model who was always seeking to improve herself and empower others. Christy has a Bachelors degree and encouraged me to pursue mine and would often watch Breona while I attended school. We often take turns watching each other's children. Surprisingly enough, Christy's son Kaseem, Anita's daughter Robin and my Breona all went to The Kids Place, Day Care Center. Ms. Eve Littman is an exceptional teacher who firmly believes in a solid educational foundation for all children. Eighteen years have passed and Eve still keeps in contact with Breona to find out about her educational and social achievements.

I guess you can say I had a support system comprised of different individuals I met along my journey that God had connected me to. But I still felt like I needed to go back home, so I did. I went back home and found a job in social services. I continued to go to school on the weekends and in 1998 I graduated with my Bachelors Degree in Human Services from Springfield College. This was one of the best moments of my life and this time Grandma Humphrey was there to see me accept my degree. This was a huge deal because I never graduated

Moving On

from high school; I received my GED while in Job Corps. Many of my family members and friends were there to support me, including my close friends Marla and Anita, but more importantly, my daughter was there to see me achieve the first goal of many to come.

After I graduated from Springfield College, I rarely went back to visit Springfield. I guess that's because I really didn't have a reason to. If I could rename the city, I would call it "Hatersville" because I have never met so many envious and jealous people in one town. This alone, left a bad taste in my mouth and was glad to spit it out.

I still brought Breona upstate to see her father when I could. But after I moved, it started to become difficult to make that four hour trip, so I would write more, send pictures and accepted his phone calls. Somewhere in the process, Anthony's communication stopped and we never really heard from him again. Even though I never understood why, I had to continue to keep climbing, and that's exactly what I did. Since Anthony's family hasn't been in Breona's life for whatever reason, they became strangers to her too. Breona never asked about any of them again. It's as if she just forgot about them altogether, so I never tried to force her to visit or spend time with them. I didn't grow up with my father or his family and I didn't want my daughter to go through that experience.

This chapter of my life was filled with both happy and sad occasions; but most importantly, I learned a lot about myself, Anthony, family values, and life in general. Anthony wasn't the wrong person he just wasn't the right one for me.

As long as I can remember, my imagination, dreams and ideas have conceived limits so far out of

Love, Baby and Life

reach and I knew Anthony had never been in a relationship with anyone who was as driven and determined as I am. He was use to dealing with round-the-way girls with very little ambition and motivation, which had to be difficult for him because I was the opposite. After I learned he wanted to be free ... I let him fly.

However, we were together for seven years and during that time, we both agreed that our daughter Breona Wennette Moore was conceived out of true love.

After my relationship with Anthony, I never got involved in another unhealthy one. In fact, I realized that it is more important to learn and know a person from the inside out and not the other way around. While growing up, I didn't see many healthy relationships; but it only took one bad one for me to realize that I never want to experience that again. Love is what you make it and I refuse to get involved in another relationship where I am giving 100% and my mate is giving less...its either 100% or nothing.

Here are a few important check points to consider for healthy relationships.

1. Always Be Your *"True"* Self.
2. Openly **Communicate** with one another.
3. Always be **Honest** with one another.
4. Don't ignore, but **Explore** your differences.
5. **Learn** to laugh and cry together, not at each other.
6. **Express** your feelings about your spiritual beliefs.
7. **Respect** and **Appreciate** your body...it's your temple.

Moving On

8. **Avoid** negative people and influences.
9. Learn to **Compromise** with one another...put the other first.
10. **Develop** and **Cultivate Trust** from the very beginning.
11. Respect the **Boundaries** of the relationship.
12. **Respect** yourself and people will respect you.
13. **Don't** make anyone a priority in your life when you're just an option in theirs.
14. **Never** be with a person just for convenience.
15. **Keep** your friends out of your relationship.
16. **Never** become complacent in the relationship, keep doing what you did in the beginning to attract one another.
17. Never mistake **Forgiveness** for a sign of weakness.
18. **Encourage** and not discourage one another.
19. Be **Supportive** of one another's goals and dreams.
20. **Prayer** is very powerful...don't be afraid to pray together.

SECTION 4
LIFE'S TWIST

ALL Cookies ain't *Sweet*

A Childhood Story

CHAPTER 14
CLOSURE

It has been my life-long dream to write a book and it just so happens that my first book is about me and my life. When I met with the publisher about bringing my book to life, she agreed that I had not only a story to tell, but a testimony as well. I had so many emotions bottled up inside me that I knew this book was not going to be easy to write. I wanted to be honest with myself and true to my readers, without hurting anyone, so before I started writing the book, I confided in the one person in this world who I cherish beyond measures. I thought my daughter should know everything about this project. Even though the book is based on my life, it would somehow have an impact on hers. Breona is an extremely bright girl who thinks of me as her hero and therefore,

Life's Twist

she wanted me to write my story in hopes to reach and connect with others.

It has always been my mission as a mother to be truthful with her; therefore, when she was twelve, I told her everything that she needed to know about me, from my juvenile drug use to me getting arrested and everything before, after and between. I figured there wasn't anything in my childhood or even adulthood for that matter, which was so bad that I couldn't share it with her so I did. I wanted her to hear it firsthand from me and not secondhand from the streets.

Breona Wennette Moore my gift from God.

My daughter - Queen "B" at the age of one.

My daughter, Breona Moore, Class of 2008.

Me, Tammie, Cheri, and Terri Humphrey Celebrating the "Graduation" of my Masters Degree 2003.

Me all smiles after receiving my B.S. degree at Springfield College "Graduation" 1998.

Closure

When I started this book last year, I had no idea this book would take such a drastic turn, and end with my final destination for closure...a final destination which would change my life forever. God was the driver and controlled each direction and turn this book went.

I remember struggling with Chapter Six for some reason. I couldn't start or finish this particular chapter and found it difficult to stay focused which was a delay in me completing the book sooner. I didn't realize at the time that this was God's plan to stall me from completing the book altogether because He had a different vision on how He wanted me to end the book. He had given me a dosage of temporary writer's block, because He wanted to reunite me with my birth mother. And because of God's new plan, I reunited with my mother while working on Chapter Eleven.

I received a call in the fall of 2007 from my cousin Darryl Williams in Manhattan, telling me that he found my mother, as if she had been lost.

My mother didn't know Darryl, who is Grandma Humphrey's youngest sister's son. Anyway, it was no coincidence that my mother joined the same church that Darryl directed the choir. When she joined the church, she stated her name and he believed that person to be her. While not being a 100% sure if that was her, Darryl did some investigating of his own to prove her true identity. He made several attempts to connect with her before talking to me, but each attempt just wasn't the right time.

Eventually they crossed paths at church and Darryl spoke with her and told her who he was and where I was. Needless to say, Darryl made the connection and we both agreed to meet. I was excited

Life's Twist

and the first person I told was my daughter. I knew she would be happy for me because of her experience of having her father in and out of her life, therefore, she understood how I felt and how important this was for me.

The night before I was to see her, I remember feeling so nervous I couldn't eat or sleep. There had to be a million and one things running through my head all at once. And I also started thinking about the what if's. I had waited thirty-seven years for this day to come and it had finally arrived. I wanted to tell Grandma Humphrey so bad, but I wanted to meet with her first before I mentioned anything.

When we met I was amazed at how much she looked like Grandma Humphrey and Uncle Fats. It was definitely a reunion and we talked for hours. I brought her some pictures of Breona and the family. I learned a lot about her during our visit. My mother's childhood friend was Bonnie Davis and they hung out together all the time and were practically inseparable. Bonnie would always reminisce on the past, and tell me a lot about things they did back in the day.

Bonnie also told me many years ago that I had a brother in Harlem, NY but she wasn't sure of his name. Well during my visit with my birth mother, she confirmed that I had a younger brother William Humphrey born June 3, 1983, but she did not know where he was. So it was like I found her, but there is still another hurdle I have to climb because now I need to find him. I quickly shifted all my questions about her to inquiring about him because I knew I wanted to start looking for him. I thought to myself William is now a man so I got to thinking if he was adopted, his new parents probably changed his first and last name

Closure

which will make it even harder to locate him. At that very moment I didn't like her too much.

As happy as I was to meet her, I had a lot of questions and I figured this may be my only chance, so I went for it. I'm still not sure if she told me the truth about everything or what she thought I wanted to hear, but I left her feeling some sense of relief and a little closer to her. Earlier that day I had wrote a list of questions to ask her, but once I got there, I let God guide my tongue and the questions just seemed to flow in sequence. Meeting with her was like meeting a stranger for the first time which felt somewhat awkward to me. After listening to her, I could tell she lived a rough life, but I thought to myself so did I. The difference between her life and mine's is she chose to live her life that way, and because of that I suffered.

My mother wasn't who or what I imagined her to be. The visions that I had carried in my head for so long had gradually faded away. Her appearance and character was different from what I remember and wasn't what I expected at all. Its funny when you think about it, we don't get to choose our parents and our parents don't choose us, but through the creation of nature we are chosen.

I am happy that God connected us back together, but I feel I was robbed of so many years which I will never be able to get back. In addition, I have a younger brother whom I never had the chance to meet and may never will. There is not a day that goes by that I don't think about him, but I'm sure with Gods direction and guidance, I will find him one day.

My mother gave birth to two children and walked away...never looking back and I'm sure that demon she will carry on her back for the rest of her life. When

Life's Twist

I met her, I asked many questions, but never did I judge her...I will leave that one up to God. My scars have since healed and I feel good about who I am and what I have become. My mother has to look at herself in the mirror every single day knowing what she did to our family and I know that can't be easy to do. I was determined to break the cycle but not to break down.

Forgive and Move On: This may be by far the most difficult task for me yet, but each day I pray and ask God to soften my heart. I learned you may never forget but you can certainly choose to forgive and move on. With time and patience, the hurt and pain will slowly fade away. It's like the saying goes "time heals all wounds" and I can only hope that is true in my case. I have come to realize that forgiving makes your life easier and provides you with a sense of inner peace. I am a happier person today because I chose to shed off the anger and not allow hate to settle in my heart. Although forgiving is a process and a part of healing, it doesn't excuse, deny, ignore or hide what caused that pain. It takes a lot of effort to forgive and the one who learns that will have learned the power of love.

I wrote this book for the following Reasons:

1. I wanted closure in my life.
2. I wanted to be totally set free.
3. I wanted to acknowledge the positive influences in my life.
4. I wanted to share all of my blessings as well as life's lessons.

Closure

5. I wanted to reach out and touch someone else's soul.

More importantly, I wanted to share my story to reach others who are currently in the foster care or state system, and/or those who have experienced similar life situations. I'm sure you have heard the phrase "**God doesn't put more on you than you can bear**"...well I am living proof this is a true statement. For those who are faced with challenges and systematic obstacles, continue to pray and keep your faith.

It's definitely okay to cry; rather it is because you are happy or sad. Even though my life taste so much sweeter now, I continue to shed both tears of joy and pain and that's mainly because I was dealt a bad hand that I didn't fold or walk away from, but played to the end...meaning I wasn't going down without a fight. I chose to face all my obstacles rather than ignore or run away from them and through all the heartache and pain ......**"Still I Rise"**.

Food For Thought: Never, use circumstances as an excuse for your mistakes and never make obstacles an excuse for your circumstance. I've learned if you are fortunate enough to live through your challenges, then in many cases, life is offering you a second chance. Success is about striving to move forward, learning from your mistakes and challenging yourself. Life is about the journey and path you take, not the final destination. You will always have choices in front of you, but it's up to you to open the door and walk through.

Think Positive: If you get discouraged and feel as though your goals and dreams seem too far to reach, you must challenge yourself and remain posi-

Life's Twist

tive...because there is no pity worse than self pity. Failing is one thing, but not trying is another. Think about what makes you happy. Remember with success comes a sense of pride and accomplishment. The easiest path is not always the right path...work for what you want out of life and it can only be as successful as your efforts.

Continue to move forward because the only way you can hit a dead end is if you stop trying or stop moving. Remember, you're only out of options when you stop looking for them. Don't be on the sideline watching everyone else, join the race and continue until you are victorious at the finish line...even if you come in last, at least you didn't give up on yourself and for that reason alone, you can be proud with no excuses or regrets.

A Word of Advice: When you're wrong turns to right and your right turns to wrong ...Turn to God.

Closure

My Scripture Resource List – Dealing With Tough Stuff

Sadness
Psalm 34; John 16:16-24; 2

Confusion
Psalm 25; Luke 12:22-31

Anger
Proverbs 15:1; Mathew 5:21-26 James 1:19-21

Doubt
Psalms 8; 146 Proverbs 30:5; John 14:8-14

Discouragement
Corinthians 1:3, 4:1-5:10

Rejection
Matthew 9:9-13; Ephesians 1:3-14 1 Peter 2:4-10

ALL Cookies ain't *Sweet*

A Childhood Story

RESOURCES

U.S. Department of Labor - Job Corps
Washington, DC 20210
(800) 733-JOBS
www.jobcorps.dol.gov

Child Welfare League of America (CWLA)
2345 Crystal Drive, Suite 250
Arlington, VA 22202
703-412-2400
www.cwla.org

Ogilvie-Carrington Center Inc.
Troy Hoffman
Atlanta, GA 30331
(404) 691-3270

Resources

Camp To Belong
Lynn Price, Founder
P.O. Box 1146
Marana, Arizona
www.camptobelong.org

From Concepts to Reality
Mr. Turner, Founder
Fairburn GA 30213
(770) 306-2627

Springfield College
Dr. Clifton Bush, Associate Professor
263 Alden St.
Springfield, MA 01109
(413)748-3623

Proceeds for "All Cookies ain't Sweet"
Are donated to benefit Humphrey House Inc.

Because Every Child Deserves A House Full of Love

For bookings contact
cghumphrey@hotmail.com
For additional information log onto
www.talent4future.com

About the Author

Cassondra "Cookie" Humphrey

A mother, a former foster child and now an author

As CEO of Future Talent & Entertainment and Founder of Humphrey House Inc, a nonprofit organization dedicated to educate, empower and inspire children at risk; Cookie knows what it takes to rise from a victim to victory.

What may have been an alternative to her unfortunate childhood, turned into new beginnings' which offered her a second chance at life. Westover Job Corps Center in Chicopee, MA, is where she received that second chance while taken advantage of every opportunity presented, she also gained self confidence, education, vocational and life skills, which transformed her into the person she is today. Several years after graduating from the program, Cookie started her career in Counseling working for the same place that offered her a new start (JOB CORPS) she also worked closely with the HR, Education, Career Development, Dorm Life and the Recreational aspects of the program and lived by the Job Corps motto: "Success Last a Lifetime with Job Corps"

Education and empowerment of the youth are priorities that have dominated Cookie's professional and personal life. As a children's advocate, she speaks passionately about education, self-esteem, *career development, gangs, violence and maintaining healthy relationships.*

Cookie holds a B.S. degree from Springfield College in Human Services and a M.S. in Counseling and Human Resources Development from the University of Bridgeport, and is completing her PhD at Capella University. Academically, Cookie has a wide variety of interest and incorporates them into her career as an consultant and entrepreneur; and is regularly invited to share her childhood story, life experiences, and accomplishments with varies social service and non-profit agencies, schools, colleges and church ministries.

LaVergne, TN USA
02 March 2011
218442LV00001B/11/P